Advance Praise for *Success Through Quality: Support Guide for the Journey to Continuous Improvement*

This book is truly one that should be carried in the briefcase of anyone working in the field of quality. It is the quality book I've been searching for through 20 years of my career; a book that holds all the key elements of the quality process neatly between its covers. In addition, it contains the human elements of quality that are so often lacking in tomes presuming to describe quality processes.

> Roy J. Winkler
> Senior Consultant
> Organization & Human Resource Development
> Delphi-E Division of General Motors

Success Through Quality is a wonderfully clear, basic review of the fundamental concepts of quality . . . rich with examples and practical applications. What a great reference for those new to the quality world needing insight regarding the "ABC's of quality", people issues, paradigms throughout the ages, the theories and processes behind continuous improvement, and outcomes, as well as guidelines for application of continuous improvement in their personal or work lives.

> Deborah Klimaszewski, M.Ed.
> TQM Coordinator, Owens-Illinois, Inc., Franklin, IN

This book is an excellent introduction for all individuals that want to learn the basics of quality. It is also a very good refresher for those that know the quality tenants, but could use a positive motivator to get themselves ready for the next level of excellence.

> Lieutenant Colonel John B. Scott (retired),
> Instructor, Command and General Staff College
> United States Army Reserve

We have used *Success Through Quality* in many ways at Ivy Tech State College in Indianapolis. We have used it to supplement other material to train faculty and staff in continuous quality improvement efforts, and as a text in some of our TQM courses. Students love the clarity and readability of the text and find it a wonderful introduction to the quality movement.

> Ray Nealon
> Assistant Division Chair
> Business and Technology Division

I found this a very inspirational as well as educational book. Tim Clark has explained not only the terminology and p
ity, but also the very basic ways in which one

D0878459

philosophy. The Library is pleased to continue offering these "Success Through Quality" workshops for our community. We are extremely grateful for Tim's commitment to providing this training for those interested in learning more about having a better quality of life for themselves.

Jacque Schultze
Adult Services Program Librarian
Indianapolis-Marion County Public Library
Indianapolis, Indiana

For those of us new to the process of quality improvement, this book is an excellent tool. It shows that by applying the steps, continuous improvement can become a reality with outstanding results.

Jann McMillian
Indianapolis Public School Principal

"Tim Clark has done it! Just like the ocean, Quality is a subject that is wide and deep. Unlike the ocean, Quality tends to be very dry. In his new book Tim gives any reader the opportunity to mentally rap their arms around the subject of Quality in a light, humorous, fact-filled quick read. Your Quality library will not be complete without Tim's new book and you will want to buy copies for friends and colleagues."

Michael W. Mahanes
Corporate Director of Organizational Development

If I had to pick a book that would serve as a practical, clear and concise guide to the basics of quality improvement, this book would make the short list. It not only is a first rate primer for understanding the quality revolution, but provides down to earth examples that bring quality to life in a way that all of us can use everyday!

Thomas Mosgaller
Director of Organizational Development
for the City of Madison, WI

In *Success Through Quality*, Tim Clark has combined ingredients from all over the world of quality into a unique blend that truly satisfies. His winning recipe of one part "What Do I Need to Know?", one part "How Do I Apply What I Learn?", and one part "Why Should I Apply What I Learn?", together with liberal portions of down-to-earth examples and easy-to-accept advice has provided a book that belongs on every bookshelf. Anyone, both quality professional and quality apprentice alike, who wants to make permanent and lasting improvements in their quality of life at work or at leisure will find Tim's roadmap an essential guide for their journey.

John R. Murphy, Ph.D.
Senior Research Scientist
Eli Lilly and Company

Success Through Quality

Support Guide for the Journey to Continuous Improvement

Also available from ASQ Quality Press

The Quality Toolbox
Nancy R. Tague

Root Cause Analysis: A Tool for Total Quality Management
Paul F. Wilson, Larry D. Dell, and Gaylord F. Anderson

Mapping Work Processes
Dianne Galloway

Quality Quotes
Hélio Gomes

Let's Work Smarter, Not Harder: How to Engage Your Entire Organization in the Execution of Change
Michael Caravatta

The Change Agents' Handbook: A Survival Guide for Quality Improvement Champions
David W. Hutton

Understanding and Applying Value-Added Assessment: Eliminating Business Process Waste
William E. Trischler

To request a complimentary catalog of ASQ Quality Press publications, call 800–248–1946

Success Through Quality

Support Guide for the Journey to Continuous Improvement

By Timothy J. Clark

ASQ Quality Press
Milwaukee, Wisconsin

Success Through Quality
Timothy J. Clark

Library of Congress Cataloging-in-Publication Data

Clark, Timothy J., 1954-
   Success through quality : support guide for the journey to
continuous improvement / by Timothy J. Clark.
     p.   cm.
   Includes bibliographical references and index.
   ISBN 0-87389-441-3
   1. Total quality management. 2. Success in business. I. Title.
HD62.15.C539 1998   98-40612
658.4'013—DC21   CIP

10 9 8 7 6 5 4 3

ISBN 0–87389–441–3

Acquisitions Editor: Ken Zielske
Project Editor: Annemieke Koudstaal
Production Coordinator: Shawn Dohogne

ASQ Mission: The American Society for Quality advances individual and organizational performance excellence worldwide by providing opportunities for learning, quality improvement, and knowledge exchange.

Attention: Bookstores, Wholesalers, Schools and Corporations:
ASQ Quality Press books, videotapes, audiotapes, and software are available at quantity discounts with bulk purchases for business, educational, or instructional use. For information, please contact ASQ Quality Press at 800-248-1946, or write to ASQ Quality Press, P.O. Box 3005, Milwaukee, WI 53201-3005.

To place orders or to request a free copy of the ASQ Quality Press Publications Catalog, including ASQ membership information, call 800-248-1946. Visit our web site at http://www.asq.org.

Printed in the United States of America

∞ Printed on acid-free paper

American Society for Quality

ASQ

Quality Press
611 East Wisconsin Avenue
Milwaukee, Wisconsin 53202
Call toll free 800-248-1946
http://www.asq.org
http://standardsgroup.asq.org

To my wife Kim and my sons Ryan and Andrew,
whose inspiration, support, and sacrifice
made this book possible.

Contents

Preface

The intent of this book is to accomplish the following objectives:

To provide the reader with a basic awareness and comprehensive overview of the quality improvement theory, methods, and basic tools.

To provide a common language and practical guidelines that will be used by individuals and groups to improve leadership, decision making, and problem-resolution skills. The result, I believe, will be a better quality of life for us all.

Success

To laugh often and much; to win the respect of intelligent people and the affection of children; to earn the appreciation of honest critics and endure the betrayal of false friends; to appreciate beauty, to find the best in others; to leave the world a bit better, whether by a healthy child, a garden patch or a redeemed social condition; to know even one life has breathed easier because you have lived. This is to have succeeded.

Ralph Waldo Emerson

Acknowledgments

This book represents a synthesis of feedback provided by literally thousands of people. To my past, present, and future colleagues, partners, friends, family, critics, and customers, thank you for taking the time to share your viewpoints.

I especially want to thank my parents, who were my most supportive audience. I also want to thank Karen Bemowski, Janyce A. Louthain, and Richard Kivett, whose editorial support on earlier versions of this book resulted in this published version.

I also appreciate Quality Press for taking the risk in publishing a book designed more for a general audience versus its traditional audience of quality practitioners and professionals.

Introduction

The starting point of all achievement is desire.

Napolean Hill

Success begins with the desire to achieve an ideal. An ideal represents a standard of perfection that one can strive for but never achieve—a fact that makes continuous improvement possible. The difference between an ideal and the actual is referred to as a *variation,* and reducing variation is the key to quality.

Since the beginning of time, human beings have chosen to take action to achieve a desired outcome. Results from actions are expressed in words (qualitative) and/or in numbers (quantitative). For example, if you were asked to describe the experience of eating a meal at your favorite restaurant, you might report that the food was good, the restaurant was clean, and the service was fast and friendly. When asked to express the experience in quantitative terms, you might mention the cost, the size of the portions, the number of items on the menu, and the temperature of the food.

Numbers are often used to help provide feedback on the efficiency and effectiveness of our actions or processes. *Any* type of number can be classified into two categories: counts and measures. In the restaurant example, counts are the number of menu items, the number of items ordered, or the number of people at the restaurant. Measurement data are derived from some type of instrument. You would need a thermometer to determine the temperature of the food, and you would need scales to determine the weight of the portion sizes.

In the 1920s, Dr. Walter Shewhart of Bell Telephone Laboratories developed an improved approach for organizing quantitative information that has been accepted internationally as a standard method for communicating numerical information. In essence, Shewhart established a new standard for numerical literacy. Dr. Shewhart classified the two types of numbers as *attribute* (count) and *variable* (measures). He also suggested that there are two causes of variation, two types of mistakes, and two types of processes. Other terms for processes are *routines, habits,* and *actions.* Shewhart developed a tool called a *control chart,* which can be used to help validate that *if you always do what you always did, you will usually get what you always got.*

The late Dr. W. Edwards Deming, who was a student and colleague of Dr. Shewhart and was one of the Americans who taught Shewhart's techniques to the Japanese after World War II, estimated that a failure to understand the difference between common and special causes of variation results in a situation where "ninety-five percent of changes made by management today result in no improvement."[1] *Management* is another term for a *process owner,* and we are all process owners, so in other words, a lack of understanding of common and special cause variation may result in a situation where a majority of changes that *we make to either improve efficiency and/or effectiveness result in no improvement.* For example, what percent of your New Year's resolutions have you successfully adopted? For those with a low success rate, do you still develop New Year resolutions?

I started studying the works of Dr. Deming in 1986, and since then have studied and applied the contributions of other quality professionals and pioneers such as Dr. Joseph Juran, Phillip Crosby, Kaoru Ishikawa, and Dr. Donald Wheeler, to name just a few. In addition, I also started to merge the quality methods with the success and learning principles taught by people who include Napolean Hill, Dr. Robert Shuller, Peter Senge, Joel Barker, Tom Peters, Anthony Robbins, Stephen Covey, and the U. S. military. Application of this success and quality technology in my professional life significantly increased my ability to help ensure that the majority of changes I was involved with either resulted in improvement or minimized the costs of initiatives that I believed

---

[1] W. Edwards Deming, *The New Economics for Industry, Government, Education.* Cambridge, MA: Massachusetts Institute of Technology, Center for Advanced Engineering Study, 1993, p. 38.

had a low probability of success. I also started to realize that the quality principles and tools can be applied to improve quality in any aspect of life.

In supporting others to learn and apply the success-through-quality technology, I also found that it is helpful to integrate the principles into the three aspects of change that need to be considered in bringing about any type of fundamental improvement.

Three Aspects of Change: Mind, Body, and Soul

Three aspects must be considered to bring about any type of permanent change: mental or logical aspects (what do I need to know), physical aspects (how do I apply what I learn), and emotional aspects (why should I apply what I learn).

The answers to *what, how,* and *why* questions can be found in the three critical factors needed to achieve success through quality:

What do I need to know?	Develop a conscious awareness and understanding of variation
How do I apply what I learn?	Adopt the lead-by-example approach
Why should I apply what I learn?	Develop your desire and commitment

What: Conscious Awareness and Understanding of Variation

What do you need to do to start down the road to continuous improvement? You need to develop an awareness and understanding of *variation.* Reducing variation is the key to quality, and understanding variation is the foundation needed to determine whether the change results in improvement.

Learning about variation will likely seem strange or difficult at first. But this is normal. People usually go through four stages when learning a new concept or skill. The four stages involve varying degrees of consciousness (that is, being aware, awake, and able to think and perceive) and competence (being sufficient, adequate, and capable). The four stages in the learning cycle are:

1. *Unconscious incompetence*—Not knowing you don't know (the "ignorance is bliss" stage)

2. *Conscious incompetence*—You know you don't know

3. *Conscious competence*—You can do it, but you have to work at it

4. *Unconscious competence*—The new skill becomes a habit that you can do well without thinking about it

To illustrate the four stages, suppose you are learning how to play a video game for the first time:

1. *Unconscious incompetence*—You are unaware of video games and, as a result, have never played one

2. *Conscious incompetence*—You develop an interest and start playing, but you don't last long

3. *Conscious competence*—You know how to play, but your reactions are not automatic—you have to work at it

4. *Unconscious competence*—Through practice and repetition, your actions become automatic, which helps you to master the game and reach this level

The objective is to achieve conscious competence and to work toward unconscious competence.

How: Lead by Example

How do you achieve continuous improvement? Once you have learned about variation, you need to apply the methods and tools that will allow you to reduce it. This can be accomplished through the *lead-by-example approach*. This approach, as applied to continuous improvement, has four steps:

1. *Learn* about the continuous improvement theories, processes, and tools. Reading this book is a good start.

2. *Apply* what you learn. To get the point, you must plot the point.

3. *Teach* others through the use of your success story or example. This not only inspires and helps your students, but also improves your knowledge and skills.

4. *Support* others in their efforts to improve quality. Finding the best, or optimum, way to reduce variation requires teamwork, since one of us is not as smart as all of us.

Military forces have successfully used the lead-by-example strategy for thousands of years. More recently, companies have adopted similar approaches, often calling it *cascading*. For example, Xerox Corporation, a 1989 winner of the Malcolm Baldrige National Quality Award, successfully implemented its quality initiative with the help of cascading. In Xerox's cascading process, leaders received training, applied the training to improve a process, helped train others in the organization, and then supported peers or subordinates as they improved their processes. As this cycle was repeated, there was a cascading effect throughout the organization. Overall, Xerox used the cascading process to train more than 100,000 employees in 4 years.[2]

Why? Desire and Commitment

Why should I strive for continuous improvement? Knowing what to do (having a conscious awareness and understanding of variation) and how to do it (leading by example) are insufficient by themselves. There must also be a burning desire to want to apply the knowledge and skills. Desire is the motivation to want to do something and commitment is the discipline to follow through.

Human motivation is influenced by the degree of pleasure or pain that people associate with a given course of action. Naturally, people seek those actions that are pleasurable and avoid those that cause pain. Of the two, the avoidance of pain can be the more powerful motivator and includes not only physical but also emotional pain. Examples of emotional pain include fear of failure and success, loss of security, and self-doubt. An example of how pleasure or pain can be used to bring about immediate change was

---

[2]David Kearns and David Nadler, *Profits in the Dark: How Xerox Reinvented Itself and Beat the Japanese.* New York: Harper Collins, 1992.

provided by my brother's dentist. The dentist knew my brother wasn't flossing his teeth every day, so he reminded him to "be sure to floss only those teeth you want to keep." When I heard this story, I changed my daily teeth brushing habit to include flossing only those teeth I wanted to keep—all of them.

To improve the quality of any area in your life, you need to break out of your comfort zone. You need to analyze the be-"causes" that prevent you from being "all that you were created to be." Change won't occur until you associate pleasure with getting what you want or pain with not getting it. This "break out" can be facilitated by asking yourself these questions:

- What if I do?

- What if I don't?

- What are the *barriers* that are preventing me from getting what I want?

- What can I do *right now* to overcome one or more of these barriers?

The answers to these questions need to be as specific and detailed as possible and written in the present tense. They provide the foundation for vision and action. Vision fuels desire, and the quality of the vision determines the level of commitment.

Putting It All Together

Three critical factors are needed to successfully implement a quality initiative. The relationship of these factors to the three components of change are:

1. *What:* You need to develop an awareness and understanding of variation. This involves learning about such concepts as common and special cause variation, the two types of mistakes, the two types of data, and stable and unstable processes.

2. *How:* You need to lead by example. Unconscious competence can be achieved by applying the learn-apply-teach-support model. First, you need to learn and then apply the methods and tools to improve a process via the plan-do-study-act cycle. Next, you can teach others via your example or success story. Finally, you should support others to improve a process in at least one aspect of their lives.

3. *Why:* You need to develop desire and commitment. Desire is the motivation to want to do something. Commitment is the discipline to follow through. A vision provides the foundation for desire and commitment. The quality of the vision determines the level of commitment.

Developing desire and commitment challenges us to identify what we want and then develop goals and strategies for achieving that which we desire. As simple as this principle seems, studies and surveys suggest that only about 3 percent of people have written goals and a plan for achieving their goals.

Why should you apply the quality theory, process, and tools? The answer to this question is a personal decision, but I will provide plenty of examples that may help you to identify application opportunities.

To answer "What do I need to know?" the book looks at the ABCs of quality, people issues, paradigms throughout the ages, the theories and processes behind continuous improvement, and outcomes. To address "How do I apply what I learn?" the book looks at the basic tools of quality and the continuous improvement process. The application guidelines for the continuous improvement and learning process provided in Chapter 7 incorporate the quality methods and tools into specific action steps.

Section 1

What Do I Need to Know?

The ABCs of Quality: An Overview

Quality is never an accident; it is always the result of high intention, sincere effort, intelligent direction and skillful execution; it represents the wide choice of many alternatives.

Willa A. Foster

This chapter provides an overview of the key points covered in more detail in subsequent chapters. The first part of this chapter introduces the various aspects of quality, such as definition, types, and theory. The second part introduces the components in a model called the ABCs of Quality.

What Is Quality and How Is It Achieved?

Quality is an ideal that is difficult to define. Sometimes you just know it when you see it. In simple yet profound terms, quality means *doing the right things right* and is uniquely defined by each individual. "Doing things right" implies efficiency; "doing the right things" refers to effectiveness (Figure 1.1). Efficiency and effectiveness are mutually exclusive terms; in other words, you can do the right thing wrong or the wrong thing right. For example, you could be very efficient at saving money but not effective if you lose it all on a get-rich-quick scheme. Conversely, you could have a great investment opportunity but not have enough money to invest. Dr. W. Edwards Deming, a world-renowned quality philosopher and practitioner, often illustrated this point in the statement: "Willing workers doing their best won't do it; you have to know what to do, then do your best."[1]

Types of Quality

The three types of quality are *perceived, expected,* and *actual.* Perceived and expected quality are qualitative and actual quality is quantitative.

• *Perceived quality* is based on what you think it is (you know it when you see it). For instance, many people invest in mutual funds because they believe mutual funds provide a higher return than do traditional savings accounts. People buy a mutual fund from a company that they believe will do the best job in helping them to meet their financial goals.

---

[1]Notes from a seminar conducted by Dr. Deming in 1986.

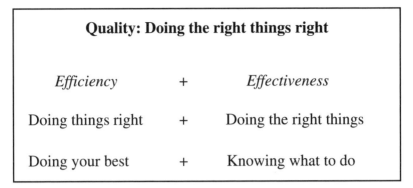

Figure 1.1.   Quality can be defined as a combination of efficiency and effectiveness.

• *Expected quality* is based either on what you think it will be or what you want it to be. If the respective mutual fund and/or the company lives up to your expectations, you may let them continue to manage your investments. However, if they don't live up to expectations, you will probably investigate other options.

• *Actual quality* is based on facts or numbers (statistics). The mutual fund industry is required to follow specific standards for reporting financial information. This standard reporting makes it easier for the consumer to estimate risks and to compare performance among the various funds.

In 1924, Dr. Walter Shewhart of Bell Laboratories developed new methods and tools for organizing numerical (quantitative) information that could be used to control and predict the variation in a product and/or service. The tools are commonly referred to as *control charts*. The methods for organizing numerical information are referred to as *statistical quality control* (SQC).[2] SQC is defined in Table 1.1.

I like to refer to SQC as *Success through Quality Choices* because the techniques help you to realize that if you *choose* to do what you always did, you will usually get what you always got. As shown in Figure 1.2, SQC can be used to align all three types of

---

[2]Bonnie S. Small, *Statistical Quality Control Handbook.* AT&T Technologies, Indianapolis, IN, 1985, p. 7. SQC also incorporates methods such as probability theory and sampling.

TABLE 1.1.	Success Through Quality Choices.
Statistical	With the help of numbers, or data,
Quality	we study the characteristics of our process
Control	in order to make it behave the way we want it to behave.

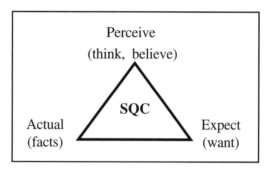

Figure 1.2. A model of the "zone."

quality. This alignment represents what many athletes have referred to as the "zone." The zone represents a level of almost near perfect performance. In other words, you think you're good (perception), you want to be good (expected), and you are good (actual).

In the mutual fund example, if you think that saving and investing in your future will help you to meet your financial goals, and you invest accordingly, the SQC techniques will help you to compare actual with expected results.

The Theory of Quality

Albert Einstein remarked that the man who regards his own life and that of his fellow creatures as meaningless is not merely unhappy, but hardly fit for life. To improve quality of life, you must start with a *theory*, and theory is based on faith. The theory implied throughout this book is the acceptance that everyone is born with a special purpose in life and that each person is provided with the ability and talents needed to achieve this purpose. Your challenge and your quality of life depend on discovering, developing, and using these talents in helping to make the world a better or more perfect place to live. If you choose to accept this theory, the purpose of life is to reduce the gap from

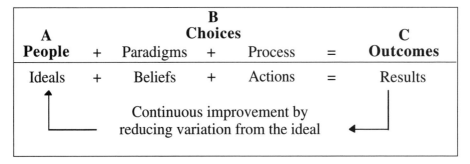

Figure 1.3. A model of continuous improvement.

where you currently are to where you could be if you reached your full potential. This gap can be reduced through the ABCs of Quality.

The ABCs of Quality

Choice represents the exercise of free will. The choices people make determine the quality of the outcome. In other words, *people* (A) plus *choices* (B) equal *outcomes* (C). People define the ideal and choose both the paradigm (beliefs) and process (actions) for achieving the ideal. Outcomes represent the results of the choices. Since nothing will ever be perfect and quality either gets better or worse, continuous improvement by reducing variation is the only way to improve quality. This view of continuous improvement is represented in Figure 1.3.

The Plan-Do-Study-Act Cycle for Continuous Improvement and Learning

To guide people in improving quality, Dr. Walter Shewhart developed a model commonly referred to as the *plan-do-check/study-act* (PDSA) cycle.[3] The PDSA cycle is based on the principle that learning requires action. In the "plan" phase, the purpose and

---

[3]Shewhart used the terms *plan-do-check-act;* Deming preferred to use the term *study* instead of *check.*

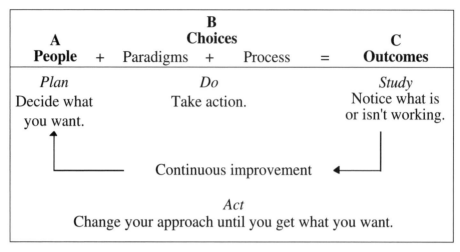

Figure 1.4. A model showing how the ABCs of Quality can be combined with the Ultimate Success Formula™.

goals are identified. In the "do" step, action is taken. In the "study" or "check" phase, results are analyzed. In the "act" step, follow-up actions are determined.

Anthony Robbins, who is a human behavior and communication expert and author of *Awaken the Giant Within,* has developed his own version of the PDSA cycle, which he refers to as the "Ultimate Success Formula."™ It's stated simply as: [4]

PDSA	**The Ultimate Success Formula™**
Plan	Decide what you want.
Do	Take action.
Study	Notice what is and isn't working.
Act	Change your approach until you get what you want.

The PDSA cycle implies a progression from one step to the next. However, progression through each step in the cycle requires choices and, generally, many of us choose not to go through all four phases of the cycle.

The ABCs of Quality can be combined with the Ultimate Success Formula™ (Figure 1.4).

---

[4]Anthony Robbins, *Awaken the Giant Within.* New York: Summit Books, 1991, p. 38.

People: The Power of Vision
Plan: Decide What You Want

Where there is no vision, the people perish.

Proverbs 24:18

The power of vision has been known for centuries. A *vision* provides a standard and represents an ideal future result. It provides direction and purpose. A vision can help you identify the "right thing."

Have you ever said, "I can't wait until . . ." "Someday I will . . ." "Next time I will . . ." or "Tomorrow I am going to . . ."? Statements such as these represent a dream, desire, or vision to accomplish something. You cannot strive to do the "right thing" without a vision of what the "right thing" is. If you don't know where you are going, how will you know when you get there?

The movie *The Karate Kid* gave an excellent lesson in establishing a vision. The young boy in the movie had the dream of learning karate. His karate master used some innovative methods to teach the ancient art. One way he taught the boy to envision success was to show him how to trim a Bonsai tree:[5]

> The master said, "Just trim the tree." The student replied, "But what if I don't do it right?" The master tells him, "Close your eyes, picture a tree, and then, as soon as you have the tree, think of nothing else. Open your eyes and trim the Bonsai tree to match the picture." Once again, the boy said, "How do I know it's going to be right?" The master replies, "If it comes from inside of you, it's right."

Visions come from inside of you. They are important for people as well as organizations and nations.

Great leaders develop, communicate, sell, and support visions. An example of a national vision was the one President John F. Kennedy announced to the world in May, 1961, that before the

---

[5]*The Karate Kid*, RCA/Columbia Pictures Home Video, Columbia Pictures Industries, Inc.

end of the decade, the United States should commit itself to putting a man on the moon and returning him safely to earth. He provided a vision that inspired and challenged Americans. As a result, the vision became a reality. Similarly, the vision at Disney World is to make every person's experience the happiest day of his or her life.[6]

Victor Frankl, a Jewish psychologist who survived the Nazi concentration camps, confirms the theory that vision is required for survival. In his book *Man's Search for Meaning*,[7] he wrote:

> It is a peculiarity of man that he can only live by looking to the future. And this is his salvation in the most difficult moments of his existence, although he sometimes has to force his mind to the task.

Personal Vision

One of the first steps needed to improve the quality of your life is to decide what you want. What is your purpose in life? What are you good at? What do you enjoy doing? What do you think you would be good at? What things have you done for other people that gave you the most joy? What things would you like to do for other people?

If you were suddenly told that you had only a short time to live, what would you do differently? How would you live your life differently? After you are gone, what will your friends and family say about you? What would you want them to say about you? Would you have any regrets?

To help clarify the answers to these questions, write a short paragraph on what it would be like if you were achieving your unique purpose in life. Make it as specific and detailed as possible. Then compare what you want with what you have. The difference between what you want out of life and what you currently have represents a problem or an opportunity for improvement. If you do not take any action to get what you want, you are incurring an opportunity cost. You are either getting better (that is,

---

[6]Josh Hammond and James Morrison, *The Stuff Americans Are Made Of: An American Strategy for Quality Improvement.* New York: Macmillan Publishers, 1996, p. 87.

[7]Victor Frankl, *Man's Search for Meaning,* 3rd edition. New York: Simon and Schuster, 1984, p. 81.

closer to what you want) or worse (that is, further from what you want) because every day you procrastinate represents a lost opportunity. Time is a nonrenewable resource.

Actor and director Michael Landon, who directed and starred in such popular television shows as *Bonanza, Little House on the Prairie,* and *Highway to Heaven,* lost his battle with cancer. But before he passed away, he made the following statement, which shows how he felt about the importance of living your life to the fullest:[8]

> Somebody should tell us, right at the start of our lives, that we are dying. Then we might live life to the limit, every minute of every day. "Do it!" I say. Whatever you want to do, do it now! There are only so many tomorrows.

Choices: Paradigms and Processes
Do: Take Action

If Columbus had turned back, no one would have blamed him. No one would have remembered him either.

Unknown

Paradigms

In dictionaries, a *paradigm* is defined as a pattern or example. Paradigm is also another word used to describe the rules, beliefs, mental models, theories, assumptions, stereotypes, or attitudes that people develop to help them create or solve problems.

Paradigms can represent the greatest barrier for achieving quality because they influence perceptions, which, in turn, influence actions. If you have paradigm paralysis—the disease of certainty—you see only facts and not problems. On the other hand, if you have

---

[8]Anthony Robbins, *Awaken the Giant Within.* New York: Summit Books, 1991, p. 529.

paradigm flexibility—the attribute of being visionary—you will see that a change can represent opportunities and new possibilities.[9]

Examples of Paradigm Paralysis

Although paradigms represent mental processes that are invisible, paradigm paralysis can become quite visible through statements such as:

- We've always done it that way.
- Don't rock the boat.
- We've tried that before.
- It'll never fly.
- Good enough.
- The boss will never go for it.
- If it ain't broke, don't fix it.
- We'll let you know.

Just because that's the way it is or has always been doesn't mean that's the way it should be or always has to be. For example, at one time, people had the paradigm (belief) that the earth was flat; there were even maps available to prove it! Ship captains in western European countries who accepted the paradigm that the earth was flat only sailed east to trade. But a few pioneers did not accept this paradigm, thinking that the earth may be round. They took a risk by sailing west and discovered new (to them) worlds. Even after it was proven and demonstrated that the earth was round, this fact was not quickly accepted. It took hundreds of years for the population of the world to accept that the earth was round.[10]

---

[9]Joel Arthur Barker, *Future Edge: Discovering the New Paradigms of Success.* New York: William Morrow and Company, Inc., 1992, p. 211.

[10]A common perception is that Columbus helped to prove that the earth was round. Paul Boller, Jr., professor emeritus at Texas Christian University, stated in his book *Not So!* that 15th-century Europeans, from astronomers to church leaders, believed the planet was shaped like a ball. He said that Washington Irving made up the saga of Columbus battling the flat-earthers in his 1828 book.

Stereotypes

Am I not destroying my enemies when I make
friends of them?

Abraham Lincoln

Stereotypes are often negative paradigms that can result in people
taking discriminatory actions that result in suboptimal (that is, not
the best) outcomes. In the area of race relations, Dr. Martin Luther
King, Jr. believed that the ideal situation would be that one day,
his children would be judged on the content of their character and
not the color of their skin.[11] This vision could be expanded to
include all types of prejudice—in other words, that one day, all
people will be judged on the content of their character and not
their skin color, ethnic background, age, body weight, social status, appearance, where they live, etc. Continuous improvement in
the area of human relations requires that people share common
ideals and work together to achieve them. The quality methods
and techniques provide an approach for measuring progress
against any ideal.

Paradigm Shifts

A *paradigm shift* occurs when old rules are replaced with new ones.
It is achieved when 51 percent of the population accepts the new
rules. To prevent yourself from being trapped by paradigm paralysis and to help identify the "right thing," ask yourself a paradigm shift question every day:

What can I do today that seems impossible but, if it could
be done, would fundamentally improve the quality in
my life?

[11]Extracted from the speech *I Have a Dream*, delivered by Martin Luther King, Jr. on the
steps of the Lincoln Memorial in Washington, D.C. on August 28, 1963.

Processes and Process Owner

We have met the enemy and he is us.

Walt Kelly—Pogo

A *process* is a series of actions that people choose to take to achieve an outcome or result. Other words for processes include "systems" (a system is a series of processes), "routines," "habits," "actions," "means," "methods," and "how things get done." The terms *process* and *system* are used throughout this book to mean the same thing.

A *process owner* is anyone who has the power and responsibility to change a process. Since everything is done via a process, everyone is a process owner. The degree of ownership is determined by the degree of responsibility and control. Control falls into three categories: direct control, some control, and little control. Another term that is synonymous with control is *power*. Optimal approaches for achieving continuous improvement require a synchronization and balance of power among all the stakeholders in the process.

Outcomes
Study: Did Change Result in Improvement?

Outcomes are the results of choices. Individuals who embrace the philosophy of continuous improvement also accept the paradigm that outcomes either get better or they get worse. For example, suppose a company spends the same amount of time and material to produce a similar level of service year in and year out, but the costs of labor and materials are continually rising. The organization either has to absorb these costs and earn less profits (a condition that the company would likely conclude is worse) or it has to pass those costs onto the customers (a condition that many customers would conclude is worse). Obviously, the processes are not being improved; something needs to be done or the company may eventually go out of business.

Continuous Improvement
Act: Change Your Approach Until You Get What You Want

Continuous improvement is achieved by reducing variation in a process. Care must be taken, however, not to improve one part of the process at the expense of the others. This is referred to as *suboptimization* (for example, "three steps forward and one step back"). The best or optimum course of action is one that results in a situation in which everybody wins or at least is not any worse off. This is referred to as *optimization* ("three steps forward and no steps back"). The desire for optimization is commonly referred to as *freedom* and *liberty.*

The ABCs of Quality and the American System of Government

The United States was founded upon the ideals that all people are created equal, that they are endowed by their creator with certain inalienable rights, that among these are Life, Liberty, and the pursuit of Happiness.[12] Our founding fathers accepted the belief (paradigm) that we all have "natural rights," and they accepted the responsibility for developing a system (process) of government, as defined in the Constitution and Bill of Rights, to ensure these rights.

Efforts to continually improve the system are evidenced by past amendments to the Constitution and new laws. Applying the quality principles to the political process requires the process owners (*We the People*) to monitor numerical indicators to help evaluate how well we are living up to our ideals and to help determine when change in policy or law results in improvement. Some examples of possible indicators include the following:

Principle	Indicator
Life	Life expectancy, crime rates
Liberty	Tax rates, voter turnout
Pursuit of happiness	Yearly income, home ownership, graduation rates, race relations

---

[12]Declaration of Independence.

In July 1993, both houses of Congress passed the Government Performance and Results Act. Its purpose is to improve program effectiveness by requiring federal agencies to track performance-based outcomes. In effect, a process now exists that can be applied to Congress as well. The state of Oregon (see Community Quality, Chapter 8) provides a working model of this concept applied at the state level.[13]

Key Points to Remember

Quality is doing the right things right and is an ideal that is uniquely defined by each individual. The three types of quality are perceived, expected, and actual. Perceived quality is influenced by theories of what "the right thing" is and, therefore, is more powerful than facts. Expected and perceived quality are subjective or soft measures of quality because they are based on beliefs and opinions. Actual quality is based on facts or statistics and is more of an objective measure. *Statistical quality control* is used to compare perceived and expected quality with actual quality.

People are free to determine what the ideal should be and to choose, either intentionally or unintentionally, both the paradigm and the process that affect the quality of their lives. Although eliminating variation is not possible, reducing variation through optimization is the key to quality.

---

[13]*The Statistical Abstract of the United States.* The National Data Book contains facts on a wide variety of areas. It is published by the Department of Commerce and information is also available at: www.fedstats.gov.

People and Quality

No wise fish would go anywhere without a porpoise. Why, if a fish came to me, and told me he was going on a journey, I should say with what porpoise?

The Mock Turtle[1]

---

[1]The Mock Turtle is a character in Lewis Carroll's book *Alice in Wonderland.*

Basic Needs
What Do You Want? Why Do You Want It?

People define quality by how well their needs and wants are met. Needs and wants, like efficiency and effectiveness, can be mutually exclusive terms. A *need* is anything required for your physiological and psychological health. For example, you need water to survive. A *want* is something that you would like to have but don't need to exist. For example, you might want a new television, but you don't need it to survive. Sometimes, you can both need and want an item. For example, you need food to survive, but you might want a particular type of food.

Maslow's Hierarchy of Needs

Abraham H. Maslow identified a hierarchy of needs and expectations that is common to all people.[2] Unless an individual's development is blocked by the social environment, Maslow believed the desire to pursue a vision, or unique purpose in life, is the dominant motivating force in people. He referred to this desire as a need for *self-actualization.* To reach the level of self-actualization, Maslow identified a hierarchy of needs that follows a predetermined order of importance:

• *Physiological needs.* Food, air, water, procreation, and shelter are needed for basic health and survival. These needs must be met before all others.

• *Safety needs.* Safety needs include physical security and freedom from war, crime, physical abuse, and accidents. They also include the need for freedom from fear, anxiety, chaos, and stress and the need for structure, law, and order.

• *Social needs.* Social needs represent the requirements to belong and be loved. People need each other. For example, no

---

[2]Abraham H. Maslow, *Motivation and Personality,* 3rd edition. New York: Harper Collins Publishers, 1954, 1987.

one can grow all the food, make all the clothes, build all the roads, or provide for all medical needs. In addition, humans initially need parents and society to meet their physiological and safety needs. As people become more independent, they also become more interdependent. This evolution into interdependency can be seen by the types of decisions made or actions undertaken:[3]

Types of Decisions or Actions

Dependent	You do it for me.
Independent	I do it.
Interdependent	We do it.

• *Self-esteem needs.* Most people want to do a good job—even if you don't think they do, they think they do! Satisfying the need for self-esteem leads to self-confidence and a sense of value as a contributing member of society. Esteem includes esteem from others as well as self-esteem.

• *Cognitive needs.* Everyone is born with the desire to learn, develop, know, comprehend, understand, and explain. The plan-do-study-act cycle of continuous improvement provides a road map that can be used to develop knowledge and understanding.

• *Aesthetic needs.* The need for beauty—which is represented by art, music, architectural and interior design, style of clothes, etc.—inspires the human spirit. Ugliness, on the other hand, provokes a sense of deprivation and even physiological or psychological sickness.

• *Self-actualization needs.* Self-actualization is exercising your personal power to pursue your unique purpose in life—to be "all that you were created to be." Maslow believed that only a small percentage of the population ever reaches the self-actualization level.

As mentioned earlier, this hierarchy implies that some needs have to be met before others. For example, if people are starving, the need for food takes precedence over the need for socialization.

---

[3]Stephen Covey. *The 7 Habits of Highly Effective People.* New York: Simon and Schuster, 1989, p. 49.

According to Maslow, people progress up the hierarchy one step at a time until a lower-order need resurfaces.

Maslow identified preconditions that significantly affect people's abilities to achieve self-actualization:[4]

> Preconditions for the basic needs are freedom to speak, freedom to do what one wishes so long as no harm is done to others, freedom to express oneself, justice, fairness, honesty, orderliness in the group. These conditions are defended because, without them, the basic satisfactions are quite impossible or, at least, severely endangered.

Governments, communities, and families represent political or social systems that are formed to help ensure these preconditions. M. Scott Peck, in his book *The Road Less Traveled*, reinforces the importance of providing a support structure so that individuals can strive to reach their full potential:[5]

> The ultimate goal of life remains the spiritual growth of the individual, the solitary journey to peaks that can be climbed only alone. Significant journeys cannot be accomplished without the nurture provided by a successful marriage or a successful society. Marriage and society exist for the basic purpose of nurturing such individual journeys.

Hierarchy of Needs in the Workplace

In his book *The Motivation to Work,* Frederick Herzberg developed a theory of needs that is more applicable to work settings. He classified basic needs into two categories:[6]

• *Hygiene Factors.* The word *hygiene* is a medical term that refers to the preventive actions that need to be taken to maintain good health. Maslow's hygiene factors needed to maintain orga-

---

[4]Maslow, *Motivation and Personality,* p. 22.

[5]M. Scott Peck, *The Road Less Traveled.* New York: Simon and Schuster, 1978, p. 168.

[6]Frederick Herzberg, Bernard Mausner, and Barbara B. Snyderman, *The Motivation to Work,* 2nd edition. New York: John Wiley & Sons, 1959.

nizational health deal mainly with the external work environment and are related to Maslow's physiological, security, and social needs. Hygiene factors include the need for job security and enrichment, safe working conditions, fair wages and benefits, and fairness in work assignments and promotions. People expect these factors in their workplace. Although the lack of these factors can be dissatisfying, their presence does not motivate employees.

• *Motivational Factors.* These factors deal mainly with the work itself and focus on developing an individual's potential. They are related to Maslow's self-esteem, cognitive, aesthetic, and self-actualization needs. Motivational factors include the need for receiving recognition for a job well done, being assigned responsibility for work projects, and being provided developmental career opportunities. The presence of these factors can motivate employees.

A Gallup survey conducted for *Inc. Magazine* on employee attitudes confirms Herzberg's theory. According to the survey, employees found these factors critical to job satisfaction:[7]

- Having the opportunity every day to do what they do best

- Having a supervisor or someone at work who cares about them as people

- Having their opinions count

- Having opportunities to learn and grow

- Working for an employer whose mission makes them feel that their jobs are important

- Having the materials and equipment to do their work right

- Working for a company that is "family friendly"

---

[7]"The Happiest Workers in the World." *Inc. Magazine.* May 21, 1996, p. 66. This national survey was conducted by the Gallup Organization and was based on 803 respondents, with a 95 percent confidence level plus or minus 3.5 percent.

Two Types of Motivation: Theory *X* and Theory *Y*

I once told a manager, "You don't get quality and productivity by intimidating and humiliating somebody." He said, "Damn, those were the things I was good at!"

Tom Peters

There are two types of motivation: *intrinsic* (comes from within) and *extrinsic* (comes from other people or things). Intrinsic motivation prompts an individual to take action because it brings joy, self-satisfaction, and happiness. Extrinsic motivation prompts an individual to take action because it brings external rewards, such as pay, acknowledgment, acceptance, and recognition.

Beliefs about people's motivations influence the process (that is, management/leadership styles) used for working with others in group situations. Douglas McGregor identified two opposite styles of management/leadership. These styles are referred to as Theory X, which assumes the worst in people, and *Theory Y,* which assumes the best.[8]

Theory X infers that people don't like to work. It is characterized by strict rules and performance standards, threats, and punishments in the workplace. Theory Y presumes that people seek joy, responsibility, and use of their creative and intellectual abilities in their work. It is characterized by flexibility, empowerment, and recognition and rewards in the workplace.

One outcome of the Industrial Revolution was the development of management systems that relied mainly on a Theory X style of leadership. New forms of extrinsic motivation were developed with the intent of increasing productivity. These included gimmicks, such as competition, rankings, merit systems, quotas, and grades. These are gimmicks because they do not improve the system that created the perceived need for this type of motivation. Dr. W. Edwards Deming referred to these

---

[8]Douglas McGregor, *The Human Side of Enterprise.* New York: McGraw-Hill, 1960.

types of gimmicks as "deadly diseases," the effects of which can devastate people, organizations, and productivity.[9]

For example, one deadly disease, individual rankings, often takes the form of performance appraisals. A destructive effect of performance appraisals is that the supervisor (rater) becomes the primary customer instead of the person who will receive the product or service being produced. As a result, some employees become obsessed with defining how the supervisor defines "outstanding" and have little interest in meeting the needs of the true customer.

Leaders in organizations that have successfully embraced a quality initiative have adopted more of a Theory *Y* style of leadership. Jack Welch, Jr. of General Electric (GE) captured the essence of this leadership style in his vision for GE:[10]

Vision for General Electric
. . . a company where people come to work every day in a rush to try something they woke up thinking about the night before. We want them to go home from work wanting to talk about what they did that day, rather than trying to forget about it. We want factories where the whistle blows and everyone wonders where the time went, and someone suddenly wonders aloud why we need a whistle. We want a company where people find a better way, every day, of doing things; and where, by shaping their work experience, they make their lives better and your company best.

Involved versus Committed

Given a typical bacon and egg breakfast, the chicken is involved, the pig is committed.

Most people in the workforce know their job's minimum standards—in other words, they know what it takes to just get by.

---

[9]W. Edwards Deming, *Out of the Crisis*, 2nd edition. Cambridge, MA: Massachusetts Institute of Technology, Center for Advanced Engineering Study, 1986.

[10]Josh Hammond and James Morrison, *The Stuff Americans Are Made Of: An American Strategy for Quality Improvement*, 1993, p. 26.

(This is true for children in school as well.) Various surveys have suggested that people often feel the system they work in requires them to use very little of their potential.

Some employees consider themselves to be involved if they just show up, while others are completely committed to the tasks at hand. What can make the difference between having employees who do the minimum or having employees who use their full potential? The answer lies in whether employees understand how they can contribute to achieving a common vision and whether they are empowered to improve their processes.

Leaders who have successfully embraced quality initiatives realize that continuous improvement is not possible without developing the full potential of employees and letting them use that potential. These leaders have adopted a new way of thinking:

Old Paradigm	**New Paradigm**
If only *they* would do it.	What isn't perfect and what can *I/we* do to improve it?

Continuous improvement requires leaders who can inspire people to strive to achieve the ideal. Thus, the leader's principal role is to help others learn and develop. Through helping others, the leader learns and develops as well.

The great leader is seen as servant first, according to Robert Greenleaf, author of *The Servant As Leader.* Greenleaf stated that the best test of a leader's skills is to answer these questions:[11]

> Do those being served grow as persons; do they become healthier, wiser, freer, more autonomous while being served? *And,* what is the effect on the least privileged in society; will he benefit, or, at least, will not be further deprived?

When a leader serves his or her employees by helping them develop and use their full potential, great things can happen. Ideally, the long-term trends of a leader who continually improves quality are symbolized in Figure 2.1.

---

[11]Robert K. Greenleaf, *The Servant As Leader.* Indianapolis, IN: The Robert K. Greenleaf Center, 1970, pp. 2–7.

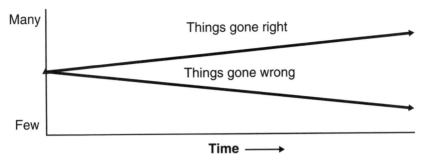

Figure 2.1. Trends in quality over the long term.

Key Points to Remember

Quality is doing the right things right and is defined by each individual. Maslow supported the theory that everyone has a need to use his or her talents to develop his or her unique potential. He referred to this as a need for *self-actualization.* Self-actualization represents an ideal future state that cannot be achieved without support from other people.

Herzberg identified a hierarchy of needs in the workplace that he classified as hygiene factors and motivational factors. Employees' motivational levels are determined by the degree of ownership they feel they have in working to meet customer needs.

Extrinsic motivation is doing something for a reward or out of fear of a consequence. *Intrinsic motivation* is doing something for the fun of it or because it seems like the right thing to do. Continuous improvement requires leaders who can develop a high degree of intrinsic motivation. The source for this inspiration is a vision that focuses on meeting the needs of other people.

Paradigms Throughout the Ages

The only thing new in the world is the history you don't know.

Harry Truman

The intent of this chapter is to provide an overview of the significance that paradigms have had and will continue to have on quality in all aspects of life.

A Million Years Ago

Early man accepted variation as a way of life. Over a million years ago, people had to make their tools out of stone to survive.[1] In determining if the stone would meet their requirements, they had to make sure it was of a certain size and hardness.

As the human race evolved, new products such as pottery, weapons, clothes, and shoes had to be developed to deal with variations in the environment. Mankind also needed such things as books, art, toys, and jewelry to make life more enjoyable. Innovations in products led to trade or bartering within a community. Bartering between communities occurred when early adventurers explored the world and found new civilizations with different types of products. New products led to increased demand, which expanded markets and led to more trade.

Egyptians and Measurements

As families merged into tribes and tribes into communities and nations, cities emerged and served as a focal point for support, fellowship, and commerce. As cities grew, so did the need for bigger, more permanent buildings. The Egyptians were among the first civilizations to extensively use measurements when constructing the pyramids and other buildings, thereby reducing variation. Such measurements were converted to specifications and tolerances.

Craftsmen in the Middle Ages

Early craftsmen converted raw materials into finished products that could be sold directly to the customer. The seller's reputation

---

[1]Walter A. Shewhart, *Statistical Method from the Viewpoint of Quality Control.* New York: Dover Publications, 1986, p. 1.

and income were affected by the quality of the product. As markets expanded, so did the need to increase productivity and quality.

During the Middle Ages, craft guilds emerged, which helped increase productivity and control variation in materials and workmanship. A master craftsman hired apprentices and then trained and developed them into journeymen and craftsmen. This system is prevalent today in skilled trades, for workers such as carpenters, masons, plumbers, machinists, and electricians.

The Industrial Revolution

The Industrial Revolution began with the ability to control variation through what is referred to as *interchangeable parts*. A modern example of interchangeable parts can be found in ballpoint pens. If you buy 10 identical ballpoint pens, take them apart, throw the parts in a box, and then reassemble them, they will all work. The parts from one pen will work in another.

If you were to try this with pens created by craftsmen in the Middle Ages, the pens would likely not work. In other words, parts from one pen would not work in another due to variation in the parts. To make it work, adjustments would be required. For example, if the top section of the pen was too long, the bottom section would have to be shortened so that the two pieces could fit together.

The use of interchangeable parts in the United States can be traced back to the middle of the 18th century. A French gunsmith developed a system for manufacturing muskets to a standard pattern.[2] When Thomas Jefferson, ambassador to France at the time, witnessed this demonstration, he asked George Washington to help him persuade Congress to try this new system in America, where it took gun manufacturers 3 years to make 1000 muskets. Congress was persuaded, and Eli Whitney was

---

[2]David A. Hounshell, *From the American System to Mass Production, 1800–1932.* Baltimore, MD: Johns Hopkins University Press, 1984, pp. 26–27; 31.

awarded a contract to produce 10,000 muskets over a period of 2 years.[3] This represented a change in paradigms:

Old Paradigm
1000 muskets in 3 years

New Paradigm
10,000 muskets in 2 years

It took Whitney more than 10 years, however, to reduce the variation in materials and work processes so that the parts could be interchanged. Due to the long-term benefits of the process, the government permitted a scheduled overrun—a precedent that's still common today.[4]

Interchangeable parts made mass production possible. With mass production came numerous other changes in how work was approached:

• Jobs were broken down into the simplest components. As a result, it was possible to train immigrants, many of whom couldn't speak English, to perform the jobs by simply showing them what was required.

• Standards and specifications were developed for products, and inspectors were added to each stage of production to screen out defective parts. Defective parts were rejected, scrapped, or reworked.

• The contracting process changed. Contracts for materials, supplies, and parts included specific standards. In addition, contracts were often awarded on the sole basis of lowest cost.

Assembly Lines and Scientific Management

Henry Ford's contribution to mass production was the assembly line. With this type of operation, employees could remain in place while the work moved past them for some type of assembly. Before the advent of the assembly line, it took Ford 13 hours to manufacture a car; after installation of assembly lines, it took only 93 minutes![5] In

---

[3]Lloyd P. Provost and Clifford L. Norman, "Variation Through the Ages." *Quality Progress,* December 1990, p. 40.

[4]Ibid.

[5]David Halberstam, *The Reckoning.* New York: William Morrow and Company Inc., 1986, pp. 80–81

addition, variation in cost and time was reduced, productivity was increased, wages were increased, and cars became affordable to the masses.

During this time, Frederick Taylor, who is known as the father of scientific management, gained fame by studying and measuring individual tasks in a steel mill. From this study, he determined that productivity could be increased by rearranging workstations and the flow of materials through the mill. This was the first of many time-and-motion studies that allowed Taylor to determine the most efficient way to perform jobs. This led to performance standards and quotas for both workers and suppliers.

The quota system for workers established the standard of "good enough" once the quota was reached. Managers were paid to think, and workers were paid to perform. This created an organizational culture in which employees were required to "check their brains at the door."

Interchangeable parts, assembly lines, mass production, and Taylor's scientific management theory produced dramatic increases in industrial productivity. These factors helped to make the United States the strongest economic power in the world.[6]

Since these approaches for managing quality and people were deemed "successful," other manufacturers, government, and service industries adopted them. Even educational institutions hopped on the bandwagon. Children progressed through the grades like parts in an assembly line, regardless of individual variation. The number of missed questions on quizzes and tests became the work standard or inspection criteria. If students answered enough questions correctly, it was "good enough" and they received a passing grade.

There is no question that the Industrial Revolution improved the overall quality of life for almost everyone. But its downside was that the resulting management system did not develop

---

[6]Lloyd Dobyns, "Volume XIII: America in the Global Market," part of The Deming Library. Washington, DC: CC-M Productions, 1987–91. Distributed by Films Inc., Chicago, IL.

employees' potential, which represented a devastating opportunity cost. Dr. W. Edwards Deming summarized this cost:[7]

> With the storehouse of skills and knowledge contained in its millions of unemployed, and with even more appalling underuse, misuse, and abuse of skills and knowledge in the army of employed people in all ranks and in all industries, the United States may be today the most underdeveloped nation in the world.

Another flaw with the resulting management system was the lack of knowledge and understanding of variation. Efforts to correct that flaw, however, began in the 1920s with the advent of the control chart combined with the application of the plan-do-study-act (PDSA) cycle.

Control Charts and the PDSA Cycle

Dr. Walter A. Shewhart's development of the control chart and the PDSA cycle provided methods for controlling variation so that quality could be continually improved. "Good enough" no longer had to be accepted. Shewhart's methods could be used to facilitate the mass production of quality *and* quantity. In other words, the high-quality levels of craftsmanship could be combined with the economies of mass production. All companies had to do was use the control chart and the PDSA cycle—but convincing them to use these tools turned out to be a long, difficult process.

Paradigm Paralysis

Paradigm paralysis is the disease of certainty.

Joel Barker

While most people shunned Shewhart's techniques, a few visionaries adopted them, one of whom was Deming. Deming began his

---

[7]W. Edwards Deming, *Out of the Crisis.* Cambridge, MA: Massachusetts Institute of Technology, Center for Advanced Engineering Study, 1986, p. 6.

career with the U. S. government as a mathematical physicist at the U. S. Department of Agriculture. He was one of the first individuals to apply Shewhart's techniques to a nonmanufacturing application: routine clerical operations during the 1940 population census.[8]

After World War II began, the U. S. War Department adopted Shewhart's techniques, but classified them as "top secret." During the war, Deming served as an advisor to the War Department and helped train more than 31,000 technical personnel on statistical quality control (SQC).

After World War II ended, Shewhart's techniques were declassified, but they were also abandoned by American manufacturers, who never quite understood the power of the new paradigm. Why did manufacturers turn their backs? As Lloyd Dobyns, coauthor of the book *Quality or Else*, stated in Volume XIII of the Deming Video Library, "After the Depression and World War II, the problem for American industry was not quality; it was quantity. They could sell anything they could make."[9]

Immediately preceding the war, America was in the midst of the Great Depression. America's decision to enter the war created an enormous, immediate demand for soldiers and war materials. Women were hired in record numbers to work in the factories at relatively high-paying jobs. Raw materials were rationed and dedicated to the war effort as American factories were converted from making consumer goods to war materials. In addition, Japanese and European factories were virtually destroyed during the war, which reduced competition for a few years after the war ended.

In fact, at one point after World War II, the United States controlled one-third of the total world economy and made half of all manufactured goods sold anywhere in the world.[10] The Depression, rationing, and control of one-third of the world market created enormous demand for consumer goods.[11] And American consumers had plenty of money because there was not much to

---

[8]Nancy R. Mann, *The Keys To Excellence.* Los Angeles: Prestwick Books, 1988, p. 8.

[9]Lloyd Dobyns and Clare Crawford-Mason, *Quality or Else.* New York: Houghton Mifflin Company, 1991, pp. 17–19. See also Lloyd Dobyns, "Volume XIII: America In The Global Market," The Deming Library. Washington, DC: CC-M Productions, 1987–91.

[10]Ibid.

[11]Ibid.

spend it on during the war, so they accepted the quality of American products. As a result, companies adopted the philosophy of "If it ain't broke, why fix it?"

Paradigm Flexibility

> The real act of discovery consists not in finding new lands but in seeing with new eyes.
>
> *Marcel Proust*

While U. S. companies were focusing on quantity, Japanese companies were focusing on quality. Deming was one of many Americans who taught the quality improvement methods to the Japanese. Others included Homer Sarasohn, Charles Protzman, Armand Feigenbaum, and Joseph Juran. Deming was first invited to Japan in 1947 by the Supreme Command for the Allied Powers and was asked to help the Japanese apply SQC in conducting the first postwar census. The Japanese invited Deming back in 1950 to conduct a series of lectures on SQC. What Deming taught the Japanese was nothing different than what he had taught the Americans during the war. He was committed to helping Japanese leaders accept the new paradigm for improving quality. He reinforced two basic principles:

1. Top management (process owner) is responsible for quality because it has the power and responsibility to improve the processes that determine the quality of the product or service.

2. The customer is the most important part of the production line. It is the customer who defines quality and identifies the requirements that processes are designed to meet.

Deming promised that if organizations would implement the improvement methodology, they would start this chain reaction:[12]

- Improve quality

---

[12]Deming, *Out of the Crisis.* p. 3.

- Decrease costs because of less rework, fewer mistakes, fewer delays, fewer snags, and better use of machine-time and materials
- Improve productivity
- Capture the market with better quality and lower prices
- Stay in business
- Provide jobs and more jobs

Deming told the Japanese that if they adopted the new paradigm of continuous improvement, they would start to capture market share within 5 years. They did begin to capture the market share in some industries within 5 years; however, it took them 10 to 20 years to accomplish this goal in other markets, such as cars and consumer electronics. The rest, as they say, is history.

In appreciation of Deming's efforts and with royalties from a book based on his lectures, the Japanese Union of Scientists and Engineers (JUSE) developed and named their quality award the "Deming Prize."[13] This award is given to recognize those companies that continually improve the quality of their products and services through the application of SQC.

Another American whom the Japanese credit with helping them to improve quality is Dr. Joseph M. Juran. Jungi Noguchi, executive director of JUSE, stated categorically that "Dr. Juran is the greatest authority on quality control in the entire world."[14] Juran was invited to Japan in 1954 and helped train the entire managerial hierarchy on how to manage for quality. Juran's approach evolves around a trilogy of Quality Control, Quality Improvement, and Quality Planning. Juran estimated that in traditionally managed organizations, 99 percent of management's time is spent on control and 1 percent on improvement. Juran suggests that managers who strive for continuous

[13]Kaoru Ishikawa, *What Is Total Quality Control?* Englewood Cliffs, NJ: Prentice-Hall, Inc., 1985.

[14]An Immigrant's Gift: The Life and Contributions of Joseph M. Juran. Adapted from the script for the television documentary *An Immigrant's Gift*. Script by John Butman and Jane Roessner. More information is available at: www.juran.com.

improvement should spend about 10 percent of their time on improvement and 90 percent on control.[15]

If you substitute process owner for management, Juran offers good advice for personal improvement. For example, quality control refers to maintaining a daily routine or process. Quality improvement represents efforts to improve an existing process or develop a new one. Given a typical 40-hour week, Juran challenges us to spend 4 hours on improvement. Quality planning suggests that we document our improvement goals to provide feedback on the effectiveness of our actions.

"The Sleeping Giant" Awakens[16]

During the 1970s and 1980s, American manufacturers took note of Japan's strong presence in the marketplace and attempted to understand how the Japanese were achieving quality. It was similar to the ancient parable of the blind men trying to describe an elephant—everyone who touched the elephant perceived something different. Some said, "It's a Japanese cultural thing." Others said, "They have newer plants and equipment." A few even claimed, "They must be cheating."

In June 1980, U. S. companies were given a clue. NBC aired the documentary "If Japan Can, Why Can't We?" When Deming was interviewed, leaders of American corporations, such as Ford and General Motors, listened and rediscovered his message. American car manufacturers were among the first to try the new quality paradigm. This was fortunate because cars represent one of the biggest portions of the international trade balance. A lack of success in this market results in a large loss of jobs.

As Figure 3.1 shows, U. S. car manufacturers needed to do something.[17] A comparison between the number of "things gone

---

[15]J. M. Juran, *Juran on Leadership for Quality: An Executive Handbook*. New York: The Free Press, 1989, p. 306.

[16]In the movie "Tora, Tora, Tora," after the Japanese bombed Pearl Harbor, the second-in-command of the fleet turned to Admiral Yamamoto and exclaimed, "You have won a great victory, Sir." The admiral turned away and solemnly said, "You don't understand. We have awakened a sleeping giant."

[17]William W. Sherkenbach, *The Deming Route to Quality and Productivity—Road Maps and Roadblocks*. Washington, DC: CEEP Press Books, 1988, p. 17.

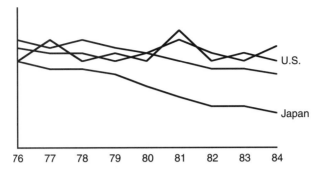

Figure 3.1.   U.S. versus Japanese cars: Customer-reported things gone wrong.

wrong" on American cars versus Japanese cars from 1976 to 1984 shows that problems with Japanese cars decreased more steadily than those with American cars. Ford executives credited this specific chart with helping them immediately understand how the Japanese were "doing it."[18]

The customer-reported "things gone wrong" is one of many effective measures of quality because, even though it might take the same amount of time and material to achieve the same level of quality each year, the costs of labor and materials go up continually. In other words, companies must get better (that is, continuously improve) by reducing the number of "things gone wrong"—or they risk getting worse because of rising costs, which are usually passed on to the customer. Organizations that do not successfully adopt the continuous improvement paradigm are putting their survival at risk. They are gambling on the belief that their competitors are operating under the same set of rules.

The New Quality Paradigm[19]

In the 1990s, a new paradigm shift is occurring. In the past, the traditional view of quality held that if variation in a product or

---

[18]Adoption of the New Philosophy, Volume IV, The Deming Video Library, CC-M Productions, 1988.

[19]There are many labels for what I refer to as the *quality paradigm*. Common terms used are "total quality management," "continuous quality improvement," and "total quality."

service fell within certain specifications or standards, it was "OK" or "good enough." If a product did not meet specifications, it was rejected.

Cost of Quality

The *cost of quality* is the sum of costs spent on prevention, appraisal, and failure. Similar to the old saying, "An ounce of prevention is worth a pound of cure," a common generalization regarding the cost of quality is that it costs one dollar to prevent a problem, $10 to find it, and $100 or more to fix it, recognizing that all costs of failure are unknown and unknowable. *Failure costs* include customer-reported things gone wrong as well as costs associated with fixing problems before the customer receives the product/service. *Appraisal costs* are costs of inspecting and monitoring. *Prevention costs* represent investments designed to eliminate failure costs and minimize appraisal costs. Examples include the following:

- *Failure.* Customer and employee complaints, warranty work, rework, scrap, lawsuits, traffic accidents, war, addictions, crime, health problems.

- *Appraisal.* Monitoring, inspection, evaluating, testing. Health examples include periodic exams and tests.

- *Prevention.* Education, training, support networks, policies, laws, foreign aid, regulations, U.S. Constitution, and Bill of Rights. Health-related examples include diet, exercise, personal hygiene.

Under the traditional view, the cost of quality has been estimated at 20 percent to 40 percent of sales or budget—a cost (or hidden tax) that is passed on to the customer.[20]

The new paradigm, however, requires continuous improvement, even if the product or service is within specifications. Everyone affected by the process must work together to find the best (optimal) way to continually improve quality by reducing variation. The cost of quality under this approach is estimated to

---

[20]David K. Carr and Ian D. Littman, *Excellence in Government*. Arlington, VA: Coopers & Lybrand, 1990, p. 10.

be as little as 2.5 percent of sales.[21] This means organizations that continually improve the quality of their products and services can have a 17.5 percent to 37.5 percent price advantage over companies that operate under the old paradigm of quality! It is important to note that the most important costs cannot be measured. For example, what are the costs of a lost or dissatisfied customer?

The Motorola Corporation is a good example of a company that has successfully reduced its cost of quality. The company reports in its *New Truths of Quality* booklet that, from 1986 through 1991, its quality efforts saved the organization over $2.2 billion simply by reducing defects in manufacturing processes. This represented a savings of more than 6 percent of sales—just for doing things right.[22] Motorola has a goal of reducing defects to no more than 3.4 defects per million parts.[23] It has also estimated that for every dollar it invests in people through training, it gets $30 back.[24] Japanese quality expert Kaoru Ishikawa stated that "investment in education pays off and can be returned 100 to 1000 times as results pour in from many different quarters.[25]

Companies that have adopted the new quality paradigm concentrate their energies on meeting customer needs and exceeding customer expectations by doing the right things right. In addition, to help reduce the cost of quality, they use only those suppliers that have successfully adopted the continuous improvement paradigm. They work with these suppliers to reduce the supplier costs of quality and expect a share of the savings. Because each supplier represents an additional source of variation, the number of suppliers are kept to a minimum. Consider these examples:

- Motorola Corporation adopted a goal of reducing the number of suppliers from 5000 to 400[26]

- Xerox Corporation went from 5000 vendors to 400 partners[27]

[21]Phillip B. Crosby, *Quality Is Free.* New York: McGraw-Hill, 1979, p. 15.

[22]*New Truths About Quality.* Motorola Corporation. Schaumberg, IL.

[23]Jeremy Main, *Quality Wars. The Free Press.* New York: Macmillan, 1994, p. 127.

[24]Ibid. p. 174.

[25]Ishikawa, *What Is Total Quality Control?* p. 126.

[26]Lloyd Dobyns and Crawford-Mason, *Quality or Else.* p. 144.

[27]Richard Whitely, *The Customer-Driven Company.* Reading, MA: Addison-Wesley, 1991, p. 64.

- Reynolds Aluminum went from 1400 to 40 suppliers in its shipping and transportation functions[28]

- In its shipping and transportation functions, AT&T reduced the number of carriers from 3000 to 51[29]

Many suppliers to companies such as Motorola are now following this same process with their suppliers. This, in itself, represents a significant paradigm shift for the business community.

In their efforts to continuously improve, many companies have put leading-edge tools to use, such as:

• *The Malcolm Baldrige National Quality Award Criteria.* In 1987, the United States created the Baldrige Award to recognize U. S. companies that strive for performance excellence. The Baldrige Award criteria identify standards of excellence found among the highest-performing organizations in the world today. Research studies conducted by the National Institute for Standards and Technology (NIST), an agency of the U. S. Department of Commerce, estimated that given a theoretical investment of $1000 in recipient's common stock, Baldrige award winners achieved the following results:[30]

> The 18 publicly traded winners, as a group, outperformed the Standard and Poors (S&P) 500 by approximately 2.4 to 1, achieving a 362.3 percent return compared to a 148.3 percent return for the S&P 500.

> The group of six, publicly traded, whole company winners outperformed the S&P 500 by greater than 2.7 to 1, achieving a 394.5 percent return compared to a 146.9 percent return for the S&P 500.

The Department of Labor has developed a series of support materials to assist organizations that are interested in using the Baldrige criteria as a strategy for assessing the effectiveness of quality improvement initiatives (see Appendix B for more information).

---

[28]Ibid.

[29]General Accounting Office Report, "Defense Transportation Commercial Practices Offer Improvement Opportunities." General Accounting Office, Washington, DC. November 1993.

[30]Results of Baldrige Winners, Common Stock Comparison. Third NIST Stock Investment Study, 1988–1996 (www.quality.nist.gov).

• *The ISO-9000 Series Standards.* The International Organization for Standardization (ISO), which consists of more than 91 countries including the United States, has developed international standards that are used to improve reliability and efficiency. These standards are referred to as the ISO-9000 series standards. Companies are often required by their customers to have their quality programs registered to the standards. This certification is conducted by independent auditors.

• *QS-9000 Standards.* The "Big Three" U. S. automakers (Ford, Chrysler, and General Motors) have consolidated their respective supplier certification programs with ISO-9000 and added additional requirements for improving both efficiency and effectiveness. These new standards for the auto industry are referred to as QS-9000. In addition, the automakers have jointly published a reference manual for using Shewhart control charts.[31] The newest standard being prepared by the Big Three is TE-9000, which will apply to all nonproduction part suppliers.

Key Points to Remember

It's the nature of competition in business today that if you're not getting better, you're getting behind . . . because somebody, somewhere, will have discovered another breakthrough that will drive the industry's quality standard to yet a higher level. That is the quality challenge that every competitive business faces. It's the challenge that every successful company will have to meet.

Alex Trotman, Chairman, Ford Motor Company

---

[31]Chrysler Corporation, Ford Motor Company, and General Motors Corporation, *Statistical Process Control.* Issued 1992, Second Printing March 1995, Copyright 1992, 1995.

Reducing variation has been the key to quality since the beginning of time. In the 1920s, Shewhart discovered and developed a revolutionary approach that can be used to continually improve the quality of any product or service. Shewhart's methods have been proven and accepted internationally as a standard method for communicating statistical information.

In June 1986, Deming estimated that the full spectrum of Shewhart's contributions would not be realized for another half-century.[32] I hope this book, in some small way, will help accelerate that paradigm shift.

---

[32]Shewhart, *Statistical Method from the Viewpoint of Quality Control.* p. ii.

The Theories and Processes Behind
Continuous Improvement

Beaver: Gee, there's something wrong with just about everything, isn't there Dad?
Ward: Just about, Beav.[1]

---

[1]Conversation from the television series "Leave It To Beaver."

Since the beginning of time, the greatest challenge in life has always been the desire to bridge the gap between an ideal or desired condition and an actual situation. This gap is commonly referred to as a "problem," "need," "opportunity," "difference," or a "variation."

Variation is so much a part of our life that we are unaware of it. This is evident in such commonly used phrases as "it depends," "it's always different," "it's not the same," "it varies," "it's unique," or "nothing is perfect." Reducing variation is the key to quality, and developing a conscious awareness and understanding of the variation principles is needed to help determine when change results in improvement.

Everyday Examples of Variation

Variation can be found in everything around you. Consider these examples:

People. It is generally accepted that no two people are alike. No two people have the same fingerprints. Brothers and sisters, raised in the same family, are different in likes and dislikes as well as in personalities. Even identical twins are not exactly alike.

Weather. Weather falls into patterns or seasonal cycles and is different every day. Have you ever noticed the similarity of weather forecasts within your city or throughout the country? Similar information is presented, yet each weather forecast is a little different.

Typical day. If you kept track of the time it takes you to perform specific tasks during a typical day, it would become quite evident that no two days are ever exactly alike.

Clothes. Have you ever noticed the differences in the fit and feel of shirts, dresses, pants, or shoes that were supposed to be the same size?

The Degree of Variation Depends on the Measurement Used

If you ever think two things are *exactly* alike, just refine the measurement! You'll soon discover that they're not. Consider these examples:

Weight. Your weight when measured in pounds may be relatively the same from day to day. However, daily variation would become more evident if your weight was measured in ounces or grams.

Distance. The distance routinely traveled to work, school, or to a friend's house may appear to be the same when measured in miles. But if the distances were measured in tenths of a mile, feet, or inches, the variation would be more evident.

Time. Time varies significantly when measured in hours, minutes, or seconds. For example, if a work day begins at 8:00 A.M., this standard technically means 8:00 rounded off to the nearest minute: 7:59:31 to 8:00:29. Nobody is ever going to get to work at *exactly* the same time every day; it just depends on how closely you want to measure it. The standard for time in an Olympic event is often measured in tenths (0.1), hundredths (0.01), and thousandths (0.001) of a second.

Manufactured products. Variation is an age-old problem in manufacturing. There may appear to be no variation in parts that are measured in hundredths of an inch, but if measured in thousandths or ten-thousandths of an inch, the variation from the standard may be significant.

Service. Do you *always* receive friendly, helpful, courteous service? Have you ever had to have something fixed more than once or had to return your dinner at a restaurant because it did not meet your expectations?

The Purpose of Standards and Specifications

Since no two things are exactly alike, standards, specifications, rules, laws, policies, and regulations have been developed to control variation and to indicate when performance varies significantly.

You likely experienced variation and standards at an early age when you learned how to write. No two of your letters were ever exactly alike; but if you stayed between the lines, you met the standard of "good enough."

Try this experiment.[2] Write the letter *A* several times, and then have a friend do the same.

```
-----------------------------------
- - - - - - - - - - - - - - - - - - - - - - - -
-----------------------------------
- - - - - - - - - - - - - - - - - - - - - - - -
-----------------------------------
```

When looking at the results, you will notice that

- You cannot write the letter *A* twice in exactly the same way

- You have no way of knowing how your next *A* will differ from the last one

- There is something about your *A*s that makes them recognizably different from those written by your friend

This experiment can help explain the relationship between variation and standards. People may try to eliminate variation by tracing the letter *A* using a stencil or even using a laser printer to print identical *A*'s, but some variation will always exist. To notice it, all you have to do is refine the measurement.

Facts, Problems, and Variation

To develop an appreciation for variation, it helps to understand the interrelationship between facts, problems, and variation.

---

[2]Western Electric, *Statistical Quality Control Handbook.* Indianapolis, IN: AT&T, 1985, p. 7.

Facts

And that's the way it is.

Walter Cronkite

A *fact* is a statement based on an objective observation. The following statements represent facts:

- The national debt exceeds $5 trillion

- Violent crime averaged 13.7 million offenses from 1984 to 1994

Problems

Nothing is good or bad, but thinking makes it so.

Hamlet

When is a fact a problem? It depends. A *problem* is typically defined as a *perceived* difference between a desired condition (want) and an actual condition (fact). Problems require a choice as to the desired condition—and choices vary. Many people would agree that violent crime and an increasing national debt are severe problems for Americans. However, some economists believe that the debt is insignificant, while some people accept crime as a fact of life.[3]

Figures 4.1 and 4.2 illustrate how facts (points) can be plotted on a trend chart. These facts represent problems if you believe that the national debt and crime should be decreasing in the long term.

---

[3]In the article "Wrong Number," the editors of *Forbes* magazine take the position that the debt is not important "until the net interest burden becomes insupportable, or unless the deficit is financed by the inflationary printing of money." The article further states that the proportion of government spending as a percent of the Gross Domestic Product (all the goods and services produced by U. S. workers) is the bigger problem (*Forbes*, Dec. 5, 1994).

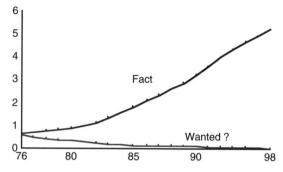

Figure 4.1.   Trend chart showing U.S. debt (in trillions). (U. S. Department of Commerce.)

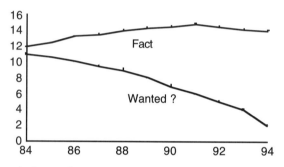

Figure 4.2.   Trend chart showing violent crime statistics (in millions). (*Statistical Abstracts of the United States, The National Data Book.* Washington, DC: U. S. Department of Commerce, 1996, Table 310, Crimes and Crime Rates, by Type: 1984 to 1994, p. 201.)

Many people choose to accept that once a desired condition is achieved, there is no longer a problem. This situation is commonly referred to as the *status quo.*

Variation

Variation represents a factual difference between the ideal outcomes in a perfect world versus the actual outcomes. An ideal outcome and a desired outcome are not necessarily the same. They can represent different degrees of variation. For example, an ideal outcome would be no crime and no need for a national budget, but given reality, a desired outcome might be less crime and a smaller deficit.

Given the variation principle, a problem is defined as an *unacceptable* degree of variation. A "solved" problem represents an *acceptable* degree of variation. In other words, a problem is never solved because variation can never be eliminated. However, people still have a choice as to what they would consider the ideal as well as what they would consider an acceptable or unacceptable degree of variation.

In the case of nutrition, for example, you will never have the ideal (perfect) amount of required vitamins, minerals, and other nutrients that are needed for good health (that is, there will always be a degree of variation from the ideal). Hunger represents an unacceptable degree of variation. When you satisfy your hunger by eating something, you have an acceptable degree of variation.

The alignment of facts, desires (problems), and ideals (variation) is the foundation for conflict and/or agreement. Generally, people can agree on the facts and what the ideal would be in a perfect world. Conflict arises from differences in desired outcomes. For example, the signers of the Declaration of Independence disagreed on many issues, such as the amount of control that would be granted to the federal government versus the state. Slavery was another divisive issue. However, they agreed to the *fact* that English rule was unacceptable and agreed on the *ideals* of life, liberty, and the pursuit of happiness. Unfortunately, the unresolved issues led to the Civil War. Abraham Lincoln's address at Gettysburg reconfirmed the commitment to the American paradigm.

> Four score and seven years ago our fathers brought forth on this continent, a new nation, conceived in Liberty, and dedicated to the proposition that all men are created equal. Now we are engaged in a great civil war; testing whether that nation, or any nation so conceived and so dedicated, can long endure. We are met on a great battlefield of that war. We have come to dedicate a portion of that field as a final resting-place for those who here gave their lives that the nation might live. It is altogether fitting and proper that we should do this. But, in a larger sense, we cannot dedicate—we cannot consecrate—we cannot hallow—this ground. The brave men, living and dead, who struggled here have consecrated it, far above our poor power to add or detract. The world will little note, nor long remember, what we say here, but it can

never forget what they did here. It is for us the living, rather, to be dedicated here to the unfinished work which they who fought here have thus far so notably advanced. It is rather for us to be here dedicated to the great task remaining before us—that from these honored dead, we take increased devotion to that cause from which they gave the full last measure of devotion; that we here highly resolve that these dead shall not have died in vain; that this nation under God, shall have a new birth of freedom; and that government of the people, by the people, for the people, shall not perish from the earth.

The quality improvement methods and tools help people reduce variation, and measure progress against an ideal. SQC and SPC have been validated by the best minds in the world for over 75 years, and are accepted internationally as a standard way of measuring quality. From their inception until the 1980s, these techniques were primarily applied to manufacturing processes. Beginning in the 1980s, the approach was applied to other industries, such as service, government, education, and health care. Now it is even being applied by individuals to resolve personal, social, and political issues. Shewhart's methods are so simple and profound that they can be taught to and applied by children as well as corporate and political leaders.

Behavior Over Time: Statistical Process Control

An SPC chart represents *behavior over time,* or trends. It can be used to display the trends of *any* type of data, including total sales, productivity, crime, weight, commuting time, bowling or golf scores, and rates of return from mutual funds.

SPC charts are trend charts with a special feature: upper and lower control limits. Control limits are determined by calculating what is referred to as *standard deviation.*[4] Shewhart developed several formulas for calculating control limits based on the type of data that was being studied and adopted three standard deviations

---

[4]Chapter 6 provides instructions for developing an individual moving range control chart (*X*-MR).

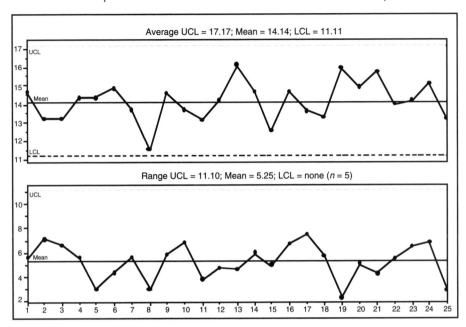

Figure 4.3.   Average weekly commuting time.

as the *practical* and *economical* limits upon which action should be taken. Three standard deviations above the average is the *upper control limit*; three standard deviations below the average is the *lower control limit*.

There are different types of SPC charts. For example, Figure 4.3 represents an average (mean) and range control chart. The top chart displays the average weekly commuting time. For instance, the average commuting time was 14.7 minutes during the first week and 13.2 minutes during the second week. The bottom chart displays the differences, or range, between the highest and lowest commuting times during the week. During week one, the highest commuting time was 17.9 minutes and the lowest 12.3 minutes. The difference is 5.6, which is plotted on the range chart to provide additional information on day-to-day variation.

Two Types of Processes

A *process* is a series of actions used to achieve an outcome. Other terms for process include "habits," "routines," and "methods."

Shewhart determined that there were two types of processes: *stable* (predictable) and *unstable* (unpredictable).

If all of the data fall within the control limits, the process is said to be *stable*, or in a state of statistical control. The charts in Figure 4.3 indicate that the commuting process is stable. Stable does not necessarily mean good, however. For example, you could have a stable process for your commute, but still be late for work every day. To validate that an improvement resulted in a change, a process must be stable.

If a data point falls outside the control limits, the process is said to be *unstable*, or *not* in a state of statistical control. If a process is unstable and you want to maintain its predictability, it must be brought into control. This can be done by investigating the special cause (s) and removing them if they can recur.

Two Causes of Variation: Common and Special

If all of the data fall within the upper and lower control limits, the cause of the variation is due to normal causes. This is called *common cause variation*. If one or more data points fall outside the limits, the variation is due to unusual causes. This is called *special cause variation*.

Knowledge of common and special causes helps you to make optimum decisions. A problem due to a special cause may require little or no action, but a problem due to a common cause requires a permanent change to the process to reduce or eliminate it.

For instance, although you may always get to work on time, you will never get to work at *exactly* the same time every day. This variation is due to common causes, such as the route taken or hitting the snooze button on the alarm clock and sleeping in a little longer. If you wanted to reduce your average commute time, improving the process would require a permanent change, such as selecting a new route or getting up earlier every day.

Suppose, however, that you were unusually late one day because the road was blocked due to a serious accident. This variation is due to a special cause. If the road was cleared by the next day, no action on your part would be needed to make sure you arrived on time.

Two Types of Mistakes

To guess is cheap. To guess wrongly is expensive.

Old Chinese Proverb

Shewhart concluded that there are two types of mistakes that can be made when making decisions and solving problems:

Mistake 1—To react to a fact or problem assuming it was a special cause when it was actually due to a common cause

Mistake 2—To react to a fact or problem assuming it was due to a common cause when it was actually due to a special cause

Shewhart realized that never making Mistake *1* or Mistake *2* was impossible. His aim was to regulate the frequency of the two mistakes to achieve minimum economic loss.[5]

New Way of Thinking Needed

In case of the commuting example, people generally accept the fact that they arrive faster on some days than others. If the average commuting time was 11.5 minutes the first week, 13.7 minutes the second week, and 14.9 minutes the third week, people might consider this normal. The control chart illustrated in Figure 4.3 indicates that the "normal" range would fall between 11.11 minutes (lower control limit) and 17.17 minutes (upper control limit). In quality thinking, the conclusion is drawn that there is no statistical significance in the week-to-week ups and downs. Although this conclusion may appear to be common sense, the application of this knowledge is not so common. To illustrate this point through the use of the following example, substitute commuting time for the average number of missed questions on a daily quiz taken by a class of 20 children.

---

[5]W. Edwards Deming, *The New Economics for Industry, Government, Education.* Cambridge, MA: Massachusetts Institute of Technology, Center for Advanced Engineering Study, 1993, p. 102.

A few years ago, my older son started bringing home math tests and quizzes with poor grades (D's and F's). D's and F's indicate that he missed many questions. I asked him if he thought the problem was due to a common cause or a special cause. In other words, I wanted to know if all the other kids were having problems—that is, common causes resulting from a stable process—or if it was just him. He concluded that since all of the other kids also did poorly on the tests and quizzes for that class, the results were common. I then analyzed where he was having difficulty and was able to help him to change his process, which eliminated the problem. I also talked with the teacher, who confirmed that the problem was common.

Mistake 1 would be blaming my son for the missed questions (to include assigning grades) when the fault was actually due to a process that he did not have the knowledge, power, or responsibility to change. Mistake 2 would be assuming that all of the children were having problems if, in reality, it was just my son. A special cause in my son's case might have indicated a different type of problem, such as some type of learning disability.

Dr. W. Edwards Deming and Dr. Joseph Juran estimated that the majority of problems in any process are due to common causes. Reducing common causes of variation is the responsibility of the process owner(s). The cause-and-effect diagram introduced in Chapter 6 provides an easy method for identifying process owner(s).

As was mentioned in the introduction, Deming believed that 95 percent of changes made by management today make no improvement. Another way of looking at this issue is that when we take action to improve a situation, how often do the changes result in a fundamental improvement, and how do we know?

On a personal level, have you ever repetitively reminded (nagged) someone about a behavior that you wanted him or her to change? How often did your advice result in a fundamental change in the other person's behavior? Or vice versa; how often are you reminded by someone else of a behavior that he or she would like you to change and how often have you made a fundamental change as a result?

What percent of laws result in improvement? For example, the National Voter Registration Act of 1993, which took effect in

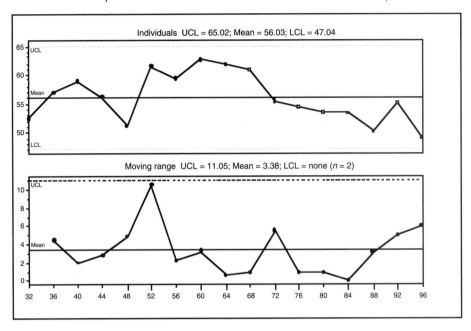

Figure 4.4.   Voter turnout—presidential elections 1932–1996.

January of 1995, was designed to register more voters in hopes that the voter turnout would increase. Figure 4.4 indicates that as a percent of the voting age population, the percent of people who voted in 1996 did not improve.[6]

What percent of newspaper headlines that refer to numerical information create the perception that something *unusual* happened (special cause) when in fact (based on a control chart), it has not (common)? Consider these examples:

> *"Voter turnout lowest since 1924"* (The Associated Press, November 1996). The headline may be true, but Figure 4.4 indicates that the turnout percentage was not unusual.

> *"Motor voter law results in the highest percentage of voter registration since reliable records were first available in 1960"*

---

[6]Vital Statistics on Congress, 1993–1994, Table 2-1, pg. 48. The 1996 results are provided by the Federal Election Commission based on data drawn from Congressional Research Service reports, Election Data Services Inc., and State Election Offices. Figure 4.4 represents an individual moving range control chart or X-MR Chart. The X-MR Chart is discussed in more detail in Chapter 6.

(Federal Election Commission report to Congress). The headline is true, but as a percent of the voting age population registered to vote in federal elections from 1976 to 1996, the percent of increased registrations represents a common cause.[7]

Reporting on the percentage of high school seniors who smoke daily, *USA Today,* on June 21, 1994, reported, *"Teen use turns upward."* Dr. Donald Wheeler, in his article *Lies, Damned Lies and Teens Who Smoke,* developed a control chart on the percentage of high school seniors who smoke daily based on facts provided by the Institute for Social Research, University of Michigan. He concluded, "There is no evidence that the percentage of teenagers who smoke has increased. Neither is there evidence that this percentage has decreased during the past 10 years. The only headline for these data that has any integrity is 'No change in teen use of tobacco.' . . . Anything else is just propaganda."[8]

Commercial advertisements are often guilty of the same mistakes. For example, diet commercials often promote a celebrity who lost weight by using a particular program. The perception created is that everyone (common cause) who buys this program will lose weight. To validate this perception, ask the advertisers to show you the facts so you can determine if the celebrity represents a special cause (only a few people who buy the program lose weight and keep it off) or whether he or she represents a common cause (the majority of people who buy the program keep the weight off). You can also ask similar types of questions to validate the claims made in television info-commercials that promote "get rich quick" programs.

---

[7]Federal Election Commission. Percentage of the voting age population registered to vote. Individual moving range (X-MR) chart used for the years 1976–1996 respectively: 68.96, 65.22, 68.68, 65.12, 71.16, 66.31, 69.14, 65.18, 70.61, 67.28, 74.4. Individuals chart: UCL = 80.156, LCL = 56.582. Moving range chart: UCL =14.484. LCL = 0. Data available at: www.fec.gov

[8]Donald J. Wheeler, *Lies, Damned Lies and Teens Who Smoke.* Published on the SPC Press home page at: www.spcpress.com. Annual percentages of high school seniors who smoke daily. Individual moving range (X-MR) chart used for the years 1984–1993 respectively, 18.8, 19.6, 18.7, 18.6, 18.1, 18.9, 19.2, 18.2, 17.3, 19.0. Individuals chart: UCL = 20.71. LCL = 16.57. Moving range chart: UCL = 2.54. LCL = 0.

Key Points to Remember

Shewhart's methods provide a foundation for decision making and problem solving that require a fundamental change in thinking. In the past, people have been trained to make decisions based on gut feelings or on relatively few hard or soft facts. But this traditional approach tends to blame people for outcomes that they do not have the knowledge, power, or responsibility to change.

The continuous improvement paradigm requires people to determine if the fact or problem is due to a common cause or a special cause. This knowledge becomes the foundation for making better decisions, whether they are based on facts or intuition. Developing a knowledge and understanding of variation will change the way you look at the world forever and can lead to unprecedented levels of quality.

Outcomes: Closer To or Further From the Ideal

Quality is doing the right things right and is uniquely defined by each individual

Author

Optimum (best) results are achieved when quality is improved in one area without making it worse in another. Since people affected by the change determine if things are better or worse, it helps to involve them in any improvement initiative. It also helps if everyone working on the issue shares a common understanding and knowledge of the improvement methods and tools.

Many organizations are making great strides in developing effective customer and supplier relationships in order to reduce the variation in perceived, expected, and actual quality levels. A common method for developing this partnership includes the following steps:[1]

1. Identify the people (stakeholders) affected by the process. This consists of direct, indirect, and internal customers. Direct customers are those who buy the product or service. Internal customers are employees of the organization, and indirect customers are anyone else who would be affected if the organization went out of business—for example, suppliers, families, or communities.

2. Identify the basic needs of everyone identified in Step 1 and identify the respective products and services that you are currently providing to meet these needs.

3. Ask your customers to identify their expectations. In partnership with the customers, develop related feedback measures that will provide the evidence required that expectations are being met. Modify and update these indicators as needed.

Table 5.1 summarizes how this method is being applied right now among the reader, the writer, and the publisher.

Perceived, Expected, and Actual Quality

A *perception* is a belief that is formed from an event and reinforced through experience. When we eat a meal at a restaurant, we experience the event with all five senses—we see, hear, touch, smell, and taste. We then interpret the experience and, based on past experiences, associate positive, negative, or neutral feelings with

---

[1]Adopted from Total Quality Transformation® Foundation for Leaders. PQ Systems. Copyright QIP, Inc./PQ Systems Inc., November, 1992.

TABLE 5.1.	**Partnership Method.**			
Stakeholders	**Needs**	**Product/ Service**	**Expectation**	**Feedback Indicators**
Reader	To receive credible and practical information for achieving success through quality	This book	To learn and use something	Increased knowledge and success
Writer	To share knowledge and experience that will help others improve quality	Useful information	To help people learn and apply knowledge	Customer feedback, unit sales
Publisher	To have satisfied customers, increased sales, and repeat business	Published books, sales catalog, toll-free order desk	To have customers like the book and recommend it to others	Sales, repeat customers, surveys

the observation. We then store the experience as a memory. If we were to describe the event, we could express it in words, pictures, images (qualitative), or numbers (quantitative).

Perception of an event leads to *expectations* that either reinforce or change beliefs. For example, if people had a positive experience at the restaurant, they might become repeat customers; if not, they may tell others about their bad experience and try something new. The factual part of the event (the numbers) is so much part of the experience that people don't even think about it.

Achieving success through quality choices (SQC) requires an awareness and an alignment of perceived, expected, and actual quality. Although these principles can be applied to any aspect of life, this chapter focuses on how they relate more to selling and buying products and services.

Perceived Quality

Perceived quality is a subjective or soft measurement based on the present. It is the basis for the saying, "The customer is always right." Customers take action based on *their* perceptions. The purpose of advertising or promotions is to influence people's perceptions so that they will take some kind of action. The same techniques that you can use to develop your desire and commitment are also used by advertisers to influence and develop your desire and commitment toward their product and/or service. The optimal goal for many companies is to provide the type of service that will lead to gaining customers for life.

Advertisers strive to convince customers that the quality of their product or service, for example, brand *A*, is better than brand *B*. Advertising associates the benefits that you will receive with a product or service and/or what you might miss if you don't buy. The most effective advertising attempts to incorporate as many of the five senses as necessary to make an association between the respective product/service and your memories or experiences. Based on factual information, brand *A* may be better, but if the customers do not believe it, they will continue to buy brand *B*. Perceptions are usually more powerful than facts.

Perceived quality is not limited to products. During a political election, the candidates try to positively influence the voters' perceptions as to who can best deliver the American dream. Negative advertising by the opposing candidate tries to convince the voter of the bad things that could happen if the other person is elected. Although surveys indicate that people do not like negative commercials, facts indicate that they can be extremely effective.

Associated with perceived quality are:

• *Perceived needs.* People believe they have certain requirements that must be met. Sometimes these perceived needs don't match reality. For example, suppose Jane lives in the safest neighborhood in the world, according to statistics. She doesn't feel safe, however. Since security is an important need to fill, Jane may be persuaded to buy better locks, insurance, an alarm system, or even a gun.

• *Latent needs.* People have needs and wants that they don't know about. These are called latent needs. For example, 100 years ago, consumers would not have expected they would someday want radios, cars, telephones, televisions, or videocassette recorders. These innovations are developed by companies that hope they can meet people's latent needs. Success in discovering latent needs creates new demands for products and services, which expand markets and create new jobs.

One of the dangers for companies is assuming that they know their customers' needs and know what the customers think about the quality of their products and services. Surveys and market research are often used to measure perceptions. In many cases, these tools can provide valuable information, but they can also lead to faulty conclusions.

Expected Quality

Based on experience with the product, if people get what they expect, they might become loyal customers until someone else convinces them that the new brand X is even better. To prevent this from happening, suppliers are quite aware of the need to introduce "new and improved" versions of their products.

When asked, "Who creates expectations—the customer or the supplier?" most people respond "the customer." But expectations usually are created by others. For example, it is the companies, not the customers, that create expectations for products and services. Deming summarized this point succinctly:[2]

> The fact is that the customer expects only what you and your competitor have led him to expect. The customer generates nothing. No customer asked for electric lights.

Companies often measure products or services by how well they meet customers' requirements. But expectations, once created, constantly rise. People have come to expect bigger, better, faster, and cheaper products and services. This concept of continually rising expectations is captured by the saying, "What have you done for me lately?"

One of the ironies of continuous improvement is that as customers, we expect positive change, but as suppliers (employees), change is often resisted. One method for minimizing this resistance is to involve the stakeholders in the change process.

---

[2]W. Edwards Deming, *The New Economics*. Cambridge, MA: Massachusetts Institute of Technology Center for Advanced Engineering Study, 1993, p. 7.

Some companies try to anticipate customers' rising expectations. For example, the Federal Express Corporation tries to stay a step ahead of its customers' expectations by accepting the belief that its customers want perfection and they want it cheap. This was the sentiment behind an advertisement in which a customer proclaimed:[3]

> *I want it on time* and in the proper hands. I want it done correctly, accurately, exactly, precisely, perfectly, efficiently, reliably, expertly, proficiently, faithfully, totally, absolutely, unequivocally, unmitigatedly, maturely, flawlessly, supremely, unsurpassedly, and certainly without fault. I want it unharmed, unbotched, untainted, and unscrewed-up, and most of all, I want it done *cheap!*

While expectations can be helpful because they prompt companies to improve their products and services, they can also be harmful. For example, in some communities, the percentage of high school graduates who decide to continue their formal education is virtually zero, while in other communities it is over 95 percent. One major cause of this difference is low community expectations that reinforce the perception that people are helpless to improve their situation.

Actual Quality

Actual quality is more of an objective or hard measure than perceived or expected quality because it is based on facts or numbers. Quite frequently, numbers are used to influence perceptions. Shewhart's methods provide a standard method for using numerical information to help validate that brand *A* is better than brand *B*. Actual quality includes facts from the past and present, which can be used to help predict the future. The mutual fund industry provides a good model for providing customers with access to information that can be used to compare expected results with actual results. Independent sources collect the facts, and newspapers provide daily and weekly summaries on sales results. Literature provided by companies provides historical information and describes the process they use to achieve their results.

---

[3]Federal Express advertisement, copyright 1993.

The Dynamic Trio

Perceived, expected, and actual quality can be found in all types of situations. They are not mutually exclusive. For example, suppose an election for the mayor is coming up in Muckville, a city besieged by crime. All three types of quality can be found in this election:

• *Perceived quality.* Some citizens of Muckville vote for the candidate they believe will do the best job of fighting crime.

• *Expected quality.* A television ad for the candidate opposing the incumbent mayor asks, "Are you better off now than you were 2 years ago?" In other words, the ad is asking, "Did you get what you expected—did crime go down?"

• *Actual quality.* Some voters look at statistics published in a local newspaper to validate the effectiveness of any changes that were made by the incumbent mayor. Newspapers often publish trends and may eventually convert the trends to control charts if the readers support this type of improvement.

When voters start comparing facts with perceptions, they also start to realize that one person or one political party can't fix problems such as crime. Rather, all of the citizens have to learn and apply continuous improvement concepts in areas in which they have the power and responsibility to improve. The application guidelines provided in Chapter 7 can be applied to help resolve almost any type of issue.

Evaluating Quality in Products and Services

One car company just redefined how quality should be measured.

GM Advertisement

To get a process closer to the ideal, you need to not only take actions to eliminate common causes of variation but also confirm

TABLE 5.2.	**Automobile Cost Comparisons.**		
Vehicles	**Achieva**	**Accord**	**Camry**
Maintenance+	$ 959	$2,756	$1,499
Repairs	$ 512	$ 366	$1,283
Operating cost++	$4,084	$4,098	$4,358
Total cost	$5,555	$7,220	$7,140

that those actions are actually reducing variation. This can be done by studying the process's outcomes to determine what is and isn't working.

In 1992, General Motors (GM) started promoting a standard definition as to "how quality should be measured." It sponsored an independent test to compare the quality of its Achieva to the highly rated and best-selling Honda Accord and Toyota Camry. The test concluded that the Achieva's average total cost of operation, including maintenance, repairs, and operating costs, was $5,555 for the first 100,000 miles. This amount was less than the Accord's and the Camry's average total costs, which were $7,220 and $7,140, respectively.[4] This advertisement helped to create a perception that the quality level of the Achieva was just as good as that of the Accord and Camry. Table 5.2 provides the cost comparisons.

GM was trying to start a revolution in the auto industry by raising the expectations of all car buyers. If GM can build a car that can be operated for 100,000 miles for an average total cost of $5,555, then all car manufacturers should be able to do it. In other words, GM was attempting to raise car buyers' expected quality level.

But do the actual quality level and costs match the expected ones? According to the commercial, the 100,000-mile test was conducted on a sample size of six Achievas, three Hondas, and two Camrys. Variation and the small sample size are the basis for the footnote in the GM advertisement that states: "Consumer experience may vary."

---

[4]*"Summer 1992: One Car Company Just Redefined How Quality Should Be Measured. It Goes Further Than the Test Track."* General Motors Advertisement, 1992. In Table 5.2, the "+" indicates that the figures are based on the manufacturer's recommended maintenance schedule, and the "++" indicates that fuel, fluids, and routine wear-outs are included.

This advertisement caught my attention because I like GM's definition of how quality should be measured. I also bought a Camry in 1992 and I expected that my costs would be less than $5,555. I estimate my actual total costs for the first 100,000 miles were $4,800. I also don't expect to spend much more than $4,800 during the next 100,000 miles of operation.

GM's comparison of total cost of use is not only applicable to cars, but also to any type of product or service. Companies that offer extended warranties have to know their warranty costs in order to make money on the service.

With such data, companies could provide consumers with an estimated total cost of their products and services (initial cost plus the average cost of use). Such information would be invaluable to consumers. For example, suppose you have a choice between two similar products: Product A, which has an initial cost of $600, and Product B, which has an initial cost of $650. If you perceive that both products are identical, you might buy the less expensive one (Product A). But what if the maintenance costs of Product A over a 5-year period were estimated to be $150 and those for Product B were zero? Regardless of your choice, you would have more facts to make a more informed decision.

Quality and Price Comparisons

	Product A	Product B
Initial cost	$600	$650
5-year average repair costs	$150	$0
Total costs	$750	$650

Organizations that successfully apply SQC are able to reduce the total costs of their products or services. In addition, they can often provide them at an initial cost that is much less than that of the competition.

The continuous improvement paradigm, in effect, provides a common language for customers and suppliers—a language that can be used to match perceived and expected quality with actual quality. This can be summarized in four words: *"Show me the variation."* In other words, you must compare what you want (ideal/desired outcome) with the current or past situation to determine if quality is getting better or worse.

TABLE 5.3.	Paradigm Shift.			
Customer Need	Farmer's Requirement	Past Paradigm	Present Paradigm	Future Paradigm
Food	Till land to grow crops	Plow horse	Tractor	What seems impossible but practical?

Efficiency, Effectiveness, and Paradigm Shifts

If quality is getting worse, if the competition is getting better, or if customers' expectations are rising, you need to change your approach. Basically, you need to improve efficiency or improve effectiveness. *Efficiency* is concerned with improving *existing* products and services, and *effectiveness* is concerned with developing *new* products and services to meet needs and expectations.

The difference between improving efficiency versus effectiveness can be seen in the evolution of farming. A century ago, horse breeders raised and sold plow horses to farmers. These breeders may have asked their customers how they could improve their product—a question to which the farmer likely replied, "I need a horse that is twice as strong and eats half as much." While the breeders were trying to develop a more perfect horse (improving efficiency), someone else was inventing a new product—the tractor (improving effectiveness).

As Table 5.3 shows, the plow horse and the tractor represent a paradigm shift in meeting the farmers' need to till the land so that they can grow crops and thus provide food to their customers. Paradigm shifts are desirable because they tend to delight the customer by closing the gap between actual and expected quality.

Paradigms do not necessarily replace each other; sometimes they coexist. For example, Amish farmers still consider the plow horse an accepted paradigm.

Another example of improving efficiency versus effectiveness can be found in the history of communication. AM radio was the major source of communication and home entertainment in the 1930s and 1940s. While other suppliers were striving to make the perfect AM radio, someone else was developing a new product—the AM/FM radio. The introduction of AM/FM radios has made AM-only band radios virtually obsolete. This continuous improvement cycle is illustrated in Figure 5.1 through a series of steps.

Quality: Doing the Right Things Right

Goal: Improve efficiency (Doing things right)	Paradigm shift	**Goal: Improve effectiveness** (Doing the right things)
If you always do what you always did, you will usually get what you always got.	+	What today seems impossible, but, if it could be done, would fundamentally improve quality?
		Latent Need:
		1. AM radio
2. AM radio		3. AM/FM radio
4. AM/FM radio		5. ?

Figure 5.1.   Continuous improvement cycle.

The paradigm shift didn't stop with the AM/FM radio. The invention of the black-and-white television replaced the radio as the major source of home entertainment and created new markets. The development of color television reduced the demand for black-and-white television. To expand their markets and increase sales, manufacturers of AM/FM radios made them smaller and more portable and added options such as cassette and compact disk players.

Quality and Creativity

Creativity is a concept that is essential for paradigm shifts. Creativity is needed to answer the paradigm shift question: "What seems impossible today, but, if it could be done, would fundamentally improve quality?" In other words, what is impossible but yet practical?

To identify the impossible, observe how the product or service is being used or provided and then identify (create) the ideal opposite fact or situation. For example, in the 1950s, the process of watching television included:

- Getting up to turn the television on
- Getting up to adjust the sound
- Getting up to change the channel (limited to three or four)
- Getting up to turn the television off

"Getting up" is a noticeable theme in the process. The opposite of "getting up" is "not getting up." So one answer to the 1950s question, "What today seems impossible but yet practical?" was the remote control. If this paradigm shift question was asked today, the answers might lead to the development of a "smart" TV that is voice-activated and tracks your viewing preferences so you don't have to spend a lot of time scanning for your favorite shows.

These same techniques can be applied within an organization in producing a product or service. The answers to the paradigm shift questions are commonly referred to as *employee suggestions.* A challenging goal for leaders within organizations is to challenge employees to create 100 to 200 suggestions per year (two–four per week), of which 95 percent are implemented.[5] This challenge could also be extended to direct and indirect customers. John Franke, former United States Department of Agriculture (USDA) administrator, summarized the results and challenges of the USDA's suggestion program in the following statement:

> At USDA we had an employee suggestion campaign, and were pleased that we got 2,700 suggestions in one week and put 2,300 of them into effect. Then I learned that Toyota implements 5,000 employee suggestions per day.

Suggestions identify either common (majority) or special causes of variation. Reducing variation requires cooperation among the process owners. The learn-apply-teach-support model (see "Introduction") can be used by the stakeholders to help support the cultural transformation that is needed to sustain a commitment to continuous improvement.

To survive and prosper, suppliers not only have to strive for efficiency, but also search for and accept new paradigms for meeting customer requirements. Improving effectiveness requires a focus on meeting basic human needs that are timeless. Products and services for meeting these needs are usually temporary. Once a new product or service (paradigm) has been accepted, the next challenge is to strive to make it better until it is replaced or enhanced by the next paradigm.

---

[5]C. Collett, J. Colletti, J. DeMott, G. Hoffherr, and J. Morgan, *Making Daily Management Work: A Perspective for Leaders and Managers.* GOAL/QPC, 1992, p. C-186.

Key Points to Remember

The outcome from a process continuously gets closer to or further from the ideal. To get a process closer to the ideal, you need to not only take actions but also confirm that those actions are actually improving the outcome. This can be done by developing effective customer/supplier/stakeholder relationships and studying outcomes to determine what is and isn't working.

If the actions are not working, a new approach is needed. This approach can focus on either improving efficiency or improving effectiveness. While improving efficiency can bring the existing product or service closer to the ideal, it will not create a paradigm shift. Paradigm shifts, which can lead to customer delight, can only be achieved by improving effectiveness.

Section

2

How Do I Apply What I Learn?

The Basic Tools of Quality

If your only tool is a hammer, everything looks like a nail.

Unknown

The majority of all problems occurring within a process can be solved with the use of a few basic tools. These tools include the flowchart, cause-and-effect diagram, Pareto chart, scatter diagram, histogram, run chart, and control chart.

Japanese quality expert Kaoru Ishikawa expressed the need for all citizens to be proficient in the basic tools of quality:[1]

> In the case of Japan, the fact that top management down to the line workers can use these seven tools is quite significant. In fact, the rate of utilization is perhaps the best in the world. Over 99.9 percent of Japanese people graduate from middle school and anywhere from 92 to 93 percent graduate from high school. They do not find it difficult to use these tools.

Flowcharts

A *flowchart,* which is also called a "process chart," is a picture (graphical representation) of a process. As Figure 6.1 shows, basic symbols identify start and stop points, processes, and decisions.

The diamond-shaped decision symbol provides an excellent source of facts (data) that you can use to plot points to monitor improvement efforts. For example, suppose Ellen, a math teacher, wants to improve her teaching abilities. As Figure 6.2 shows, she can plot whether her students met the class objectives to monitor her progress.

In a perfect process, there would be no need for decisions. For example, if Ellen's students always met the class objectives, the decision step in the process wouldn't be needed. The flowchart could go from "Give Quiz" directly to "End" since there would be no variation. But, in reality, variation exists in all processes, and as a result, there are literally hundreds to thousands of decisions to be made every day. The people closest to a process are in the best position to make those decisions and, hence, should be empowered to do so.

---

[1]Kaoru Ishikawa, *What Is Total Quality Control?* Englewood Cliffs, NJ: Prentice-Hall, Inc., 1985, p. 199. Ishikawa defined these tools as: cause and effect diagram, check sheet, control charts, scatter diagram, Pareto chart, stratification chart, and histogram.

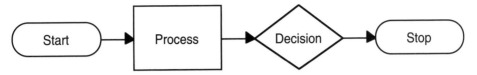

Figure 6.1.   Basic flowcharting symbols.

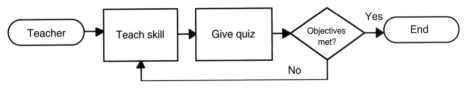

Figure 6.2.   Flowchart for teaching a skill.

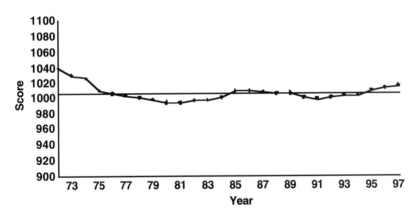

Figure 6.3.   National mean SAT/SAT I scores. The maximum score is 1600.

Run Charts

A *run chart*, which is also referred to as a "trend chart," identifies outcomes from a process over time. It provides an initial indication of whether a process is getting better, getting worse, or staying about the same.

For example, an indicator that is commonly used to measure the effectiveness of schools is the Scholastic Assessment Test (SAT). Figure 6.3 provides a trend chart of average SAT/SAT I scores from 1972 to 1997.[2]

---

[2]*1997 College-Bound Seniors; A Profile of SAT Program Test Takers,* The College Board. In 1995, the College Board recentered the score for all tests in the SAT program.

Histograms

Over a century ago, mathematicians found that statistics recorded in large numbers tended to fall into definite patterns. Such patterns, referred to as "normal" patterns or distributions, resembled a bell-shaped curve. The curve is referred to as a "normal" distribution curve. The *histogram* identifies the shape of the distribution (normal or abnormal), the spread of results (wide or narrow), and the location of the average.

To illustrate the normal curve and to provide an example of how to develop a histogram, let's say that you want to record the number of minutes it takes to commute to work each day. The first day, it takes you 9 minutes, so you plot this data point on a horizontal scale:

```
                              x
        ───────────────────────────────────
        2–4      5–6     7–8    9–10    11–12
```

On the second day, your commute takes 9.5 minutes, so this data point is added:

```
                              x
                              x
        ───────────────────────────────────
        2–4      5–6     7–8    9–10    11–12
```

As the commute times for each day are plotted, a shape or distribution emerges. Notice how most data gather near the center and how the shape tends to taper off away from the center:

```
                     x
                     x       x
              x      x       x
        x     x      x       x       x
        ───────────────────────────────────
        2–4   5–6   7–8     9–10    11–12
```

When the *x*'s are replaced with bars, a frequency distribution called a *histogram* emerges (Figure 6.4). This can also be shown as a distribution curve with upper and lower control limits added (Figure 6.5).

Dr. Walter A. Shewhart discovered that, although not all data from a process fall into a normal distribution, the averages generated from a stable distribution always provide a normal distribution.[3] In other words, if you plot your daily commuting time, the

---

[3]John McConnell, *Analysis and Control of Variation*, 3rd edition. Manly Vale, New South Wales, Australia: Delaware Books, 1987, p. 25.

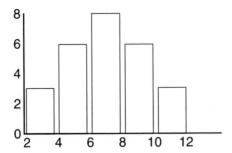

Figure 6.4.   Histogram.

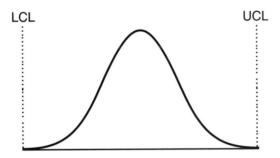

Figure 6.5.   Distribution curve.

distribution may not appear to be normal, but if you record your average weekly commuting time, this distribution will tend to be normal.

A histogram is often used in conjunction with run or control charts because numbers displayed only on a run/control chart can be deceiving. For example, suppose two groups of 10 students, Group *1* and Group *2*, are given a math test. In Group *1*, two students receive A's, two receive B's, two receive C's, two receive D's, and two receive F's. In Group *2*, all 10 students receive C's. If you simply compare the averages of these two groups, they appear to be identical; both groups had an average score of C. But the results from Group *2* represent a higher degree of predictability. The more predictable a process, the easier it is to test the effects of a change on it.

Cause-and-Effect Diagrams

The *cause-and-effect diagram,* also referred to as the "Ishikawa Diagram" because it was developed by Kaoru Ishikawa, graphically represents the relationship between an effect and all possible causes. (Why don't we always get perfect results? Be-"cause". . .) Each cause or reason for imperfection is a source of variation. Causes are usually grouped into major categories to identify sources of variation. The categories typically include:

- *People*—Anyone involved with the process

- *Methods*—How the process is performed and the specific requirements for doing it, such as policies, procedures, rules, regulations, and laws

- *Machines*—Any equipment, computers, tools, etc., required to accomplish the job

- *Materials*—Raw materials, parts, pens, paper, etc., used to produce the final product

- *Measurements*—Data generated from the process that are used to evaluate its quality

- *Environment*—The conditions, such as location, time, temperature, and culture, in which the process operates

A cause-and-effect diagram for improving the results of a test in school might look like the diagram in Figure 6.6.

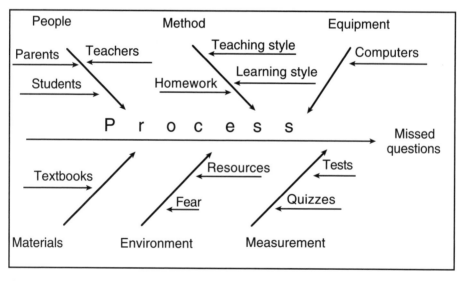

Figure 6.6.   Cause-and-effect diagram for test.

Each cause is a source of variation that can be classified into one of three categories: (1) causes over which you have direct control, (2) causes over which you have some control, or (3) causes over which you have little or no control. After you classify the causes, another option is to assign an individual's name to the cause. This will help identify the people you need to involve or people who might be impacted by any changes you make to the process. It is recommended that you first reduce the causes that you can directly control. These causes also provide a starting point for defining the problem. For example, suppose Ellen, the math teacher, thinks that homework is a cause of variation in her students' test scores. A problem statement or improvement theory may be: *If* more homework assignments are given, *then* students will miss fewer test questions.

Typically, a cause-and-effect diagram is used to identify the causes of a problem, such as "missed questions." This tool, however, can also be used to identify resources needed to implement a solution to a problem. For example, suppose Ellen determines that her students can improve their test scores if they use a math software program in class. The software program then becomes the "effect," and the major categories (such as people, method, equipment, materials, environment, and measurement) can be used to identify factors that need to be considered when selecting the software.

Pareto Charts

The *Pareto chart* was developed in 1950 by J. M Juran, who named it after Italian sociologist and economist Vilfredo Pareto, proponent of the theory that most results come from a few causes. He noted that approximately 80 percent of the wealth in Italy was controlled by 20 percent of the citizens. The 80 percent/20 percent theory has been repeatedly tested and validated in the business world. It has been used to predict various effects and their causes, such as:

- Approximately 80 percent of sales come from 20 percent of the customers

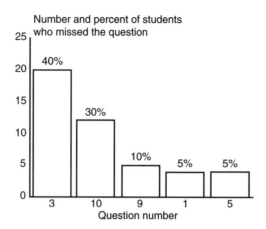

Figure 6.7. Pareto chart of missed questions on a test.

- Approximately 80 percent of the work is done by 20 percent of the employees
- Approximately 80 percent of problems come from 20 percent of the causes

For example, the Pareto chart in Figure 6.7 lists the most frequently missed questions on a 15-question test. Questions 3, 10, and 9 account for 80 percent of the missed questions.

Scatter Diagrams

A *scatter diagram* shows the relationship between two variables. It is often used to help determine whether there is a relationship, or correlation, between a problem (effect) and a possible solution (cause). The correlation can be positive, negative, or nonexistent. Although a scatter diagram does not prove a cause-and-effect relationship exists, it does help identify improvement theories that can be validated through the use of a control chart.

A scatter diagram showing a positive correlation would look similar to the one in Figure 6.8.

This diagram shows that the more homework assignments are completed, the higher number of right answers are scored on the test. In other words, it indicates that the method to correct the problem has resulted in improvement.

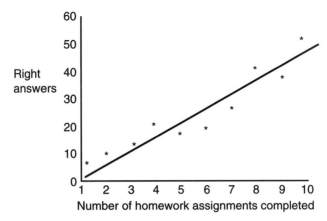

Figure 6.8.   Scatter diagram showing a positive correlation.

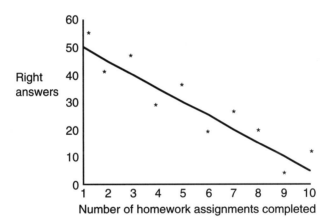

Figure 6.9.   Scatter diagram showing a negative correlation.

A scatter diagram showing a negative correlation would look similar to the one in Figure 6.9.

This diagram shows that the more homework assignments are completed, the fewer number of right answers are given on the test. In other words, it indicates that the method to correct the problem may have actually caused the problem to worsen.

A scatter diagram showing no correlation would look similar to the one in Figure 6.10. This diagram indicates that the method to correct the problem did not indicate improvement.

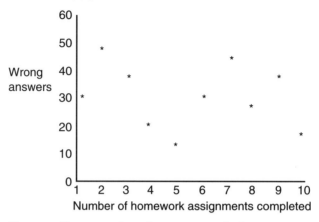

Figure 6.10. Scatter diagram showing no correlation.

Control Charts and Two Types of Data

Control charts are run charts with control limits. They are used to identify the trends of facts or numbers (statistics). Shewhart determined that statistics fall into two categories: attribute data and variable data.

Attribute data can be classified and counted. Examples include information that can be classified as yes or no, true or false, pass or fail, or go or no-go. Examples of attribute data include:

Process	Attribute	Count/Ratio
Flipping coins	Heads or tails	Number of heads or tails
Employment	Employed or unemployed	Number of employed or unemployed
Graduation	Graduated or dropped out	Number of graduates or dropouts
Sport contests	Won or lost	Number of wins or losses
Lotteries	Won or lost	Number of winning or losing tickets

Variable data cannot be classified, but they can be expressed in measurements. Examples include the following:

Characteristic	Measurement
Height	Feet, inches, centimeters, or millimeters
Weight	Pounds, ounces, or grams
Time	Years, days, hours, or minutes

There are different types of control charts for attribute and variable data. Shewhart developed formulas for calculating control limits based on the type of chart used. Matching the right chart to the data being studied helps to minimize making one of two mistakes when changing a process (see Chapter 4, Two Types of Mistakes).

Control Charts for Attribute Data

Attribute control charts are used to monitor the *count* or percentage of things gone either right or wrong. The most common types of attribute charts are:

• *The c chart.* The count, or *c*, chart records how many times a certain instance occurs over time when the characteristic being counted can theoretically occur an unlimited number of times. For example, a *c* chart could be made to record the number of phone calls received by a mail-order company in a day or to record the number of car accidents in a week.

• *The u chart.* The *u* chart is used to count things by units and can be used when sample sizes are constant or variable. If the unit being analyzed is a test in school, the count would include the number of questions answered right or wrong. If subgroups vary more than 25 percent, special calculations are required.

• *The np chart.* The number-of-affected-units, or *np*, chart records the number of defective units found per sample when sample sizes are constant. In a school example, a chart could be developed to record the number of missed questions on a weekly test consisting of 50 questions. Another example would be to chart the number of invoices with mistakes every week out of a sample of 100.

• *The p chart.* Used when sample sizes are constant or variable, the percent, or *p*, chart records the percentage of units found per sample. If subgroups vary more than 25 percent, special calculations are required. In the school example, the chart could be used to plot the percentage of right/wrong answers on a test. Essentially, the *np* and *p* charts show the same information—that is, they give information on how the process is varying—but their methods differ (count versus percentage).

Constructing attribute charts is a fairly easy task. You just need to plot the points. For example, if constructing a *c* chart, you simply plot the number of phone calls received. The control limits for attribute charts follow standard practice: the upper control limit (UCL) is put three standard deviations above the average, while the lower control limit (LCL) is put three standard deviations below the average.

Control Charts for Variable Data

Variable control charts, used when a characteristic needs to be *measured,* require that two charts be developed. One chart is used to monitor the variation in the average value (usually called the *mean* or *X*-bar value) of the characteristic being measured, and one chart measures the range (*R* value) from the mean. The mean and range are calculated from samples within subgroups of data. The three most common types of variables charts include the average and range, the median and range, and the average and standard deviation.[4]

A control chart that can be used for either attribute and variable data in which the subgroup size is one is referred to as an *individual moving range chart* or *X*-MR. This chart is used for individual measures such as commuting time, body weight, sales figures, percent of total income invested in a savings account, miles per gallon, and crime statistics. This chart was used for the examples provided in Chapter 4.

The following chart provides sample data that will be used to illustrate the steps involved in developing *X*-MR charts.[5]

---

[4]QIP Inc./ Productivity Quality (PQ) Systems Inc. Improvement Tools: Variable Charts, p. 1, QIP Inc./PQ Systems Inc., V-2 revised 8/2/91

[5]The amount of data required for calculating control limits varies with the type of chart being used. Generally, 15–25 data points are recommended before calculating control limits. However, when limited data is available (see examples in Chapter 4), control limits can be calculated using less data. For more information, I recommend the books: *Short Run SPC* and *Understanding Statistical Process Control* by Donald J. Wheeler, published by SPC Press, Knoxville, TN.

Sample Data

		Individuals Measure	Moving Range
	1.	20	
	2.	25	5
	3.	18	7
	4.	16	2
	5.	18	2
Total		97	16
Average		19.4	4

Here are the steps to create an X-MR chart:

Step 1. Calculate the average for the individuals measures. To calculate the average, you add the individuals measures together. This sum is then divided by the number of measures. For the data just given, the average is:

$$\frac{20+25+18+16+18}{5} = \frac{97}{5} = 19.4$$

Step 2. Calculate the moving range. The moving range is the difference between the consecutive readings expressed in positive numbers. For example, the difference between the first individuals measure of 20 and the second of 25 is 5. The difference between the second measure of 25 and the third of 18 is 7, etc.

Step 3. Calculate the average of the moving range values. To calculate the average, you add the moving range values together. This sum is then divided by the number of values. In the example data, the average of the moving range is:

$$\frac{5+7+2+2}{4} = \frac{16}{4} = 4$$

Step 4. Calculate the control limits for the individuals graph. To calculate the upper control limit (UCL) for the individuals graph:

• Determine the appropriate weighting factor. The weighting factor, which depends on the size of the moving range subgroup, is obtained from published tables. For the X-MR chart, the appropriate weighting factor is 2.66.

• Multiply the appropriate weighting factor times the average of the moving range (this was calculated in Step 3). In other words, $2.66 \times 4 = 10.64$.

• Add the sum just determined to the individuals average (this was calculated in Step 1). In other words, $10.64 + 19.4 = 30.04$. This number is then rounded off to 30.0, which is the upper control limit.

This UCL calculation is often expressed using the following formula:

UCL = Individuals Average + (Weighting Factor × MR Average)

Or, in the case of this example:

$$UCL = 19.4 + (2.66 \times 4)$$
$$UCL = 19.4 + 10.64$$
$$UCL = 30.0 \text{ (rounded)}$$

To calculate the lower control limit (LCL) for the individuals graph:

• Determine the appropriate weighting factor. Since the same data are used, this factor will be the same as the one used to calculate the UCL (2.66).

• Multiply the appropriate weighting factor times the average of the moving range (this was calculated in Step 3). In other words, $2.66 \times 4 = 10.64$.

• Subtract the sum just determined from the individuals average (this was calculated in step 1). In other words, $19.4 - 10.64 = 8.76$. This number is then rounded off to 8.8, which is the lower control limit.

This LCL calculation is often expressed using the following formula:

LCL = Individuals Average − (Weighting Factor × MR Average)

Or, in the case of this example:

$$LCL = 19.4 - (2.66 \times 4)$$
$$LCL = 19.4 - 10.64$$
$$LCL = 8.8 \text{ (rounded)}$$

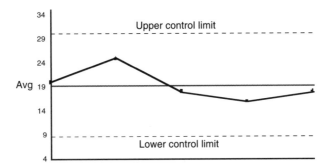

Figure 6.11.   Control chart for the individuals measure.

After the UCL and LCL are calculated, they can be plotted, along with the individuals average, on the individuals graph. Figure 6.11 shows this graph for the example data.

Step 5. Calculate the control limits for the moving range graph. To calculate the UCL of the moving range graph:

• Determine the appropriate weighting factor. Once again, the weighting factor depends on the size of the moving range subgroup and is obtained from published tables. There are different tables for individuals and moving range graphs. The appropriate weighting factor for the individual moving range graph is 3.267.

• Multiply the appropriate weighting factor times the average of the moving range (this was calculated in Step 3). In other words, $3.267 \times 4 = 13.07$. This number is then rounded to 13.1, which is the upper control limit.

This UCL calculation is often expressed using the following formula:

$$UCL = \text{Weighting Factor} \times \text{MR Average}$$

Or, in the case of this example:

$$UCL = 3.267 \times 4$$
$$UCL = 13.1$$

No calculations are necessary to determine the LCL of the moving range graph. The lower control limit is always zero.

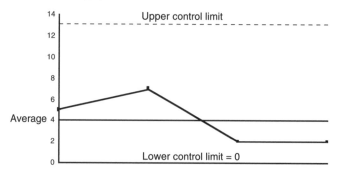

Figure 6.12. Control chart for the moving range.

After the UCL and LCL are calculated, they can be plotted, along with the moving range average, on the moving range graph. Figure 6.12 shows this graph for the example data.

The standard method for displaying variable control charts is to place the individuals chart over the moving range chart.

Control Chart Interpretation

What do you do with the X-MR control chart you've constructed? While Chapter 7 discusses the process improvement cycle in much more detail, here is an overview of how this chart can be used to monitor improvement efforts:

Step 1. Analyze the chart to see if there are any special causes based on the following conditions.[6]

- Any point outside the control limits

- Run of seven points to include seven or more points in a row above or below the center line; seven or more points in a row going in one direction, up or down

- Any nonrandom patterns to include: too close to the average; too far from the average; cycles

---

[6]There are several out-of-control test options to include: Automotive Industry Action Group (AIAG) tests, AT&T tests, Duncan's tests, Gitlow's Attributes and Variables tests, Hughes' tests, Juran's tests, and Western Electric Zone tests. The examples used in this text are based on AIAG tests.

If special causes exist, it means the process is unstable. Thus, you need to go to Step 2. If the patterns indicate only common causes, you can go to Step 3.

Step 2. Investigate the special causes of variation and remove them if they can recur. Validating an improvement action requires a stable process. If the special cause is an expected consequence of an improvement action, go to Step 4; otherwise the special cause needs to be identified and removed.[7] This is best accomplished by the people closest to the process.

Step 3. Reduce common causes of variation. Common cause variation can be reduced by:

- Identifying some of the reasons why the process isn't perfect (causes of variation)

- Selecting a cause that you have the power and responsibility to change

- Developing and implementing a change that will reduce or eliminate that cause

- Collecting additional data to validate if the change resulted in an improvement. A trend of seven or more consecutive points up or down, or seven or more consecutive points above or below the average, can indicate a change in the process.

Step 4. Monitor the process to ensure improvement is maintained. There is an important difference between validating whether the change resulted in improvement and monitoring the process to ensure that improvement is maintained. For example, suppose you decided to change routes to improve your commuting time, after which you plotted your commute times for another seven days. As Figure 6.13 shows, there was a process shift, which is indicated by seven points in a row below the average (points 26–32). At this point, you have validated that the change resulted in improvement. To ensure that the improvement is maintained, you would need to continue to monitor the process.

---

[7]Although you can improve an unstable process, technically, you can not validate the change you made resulted in the improvement.

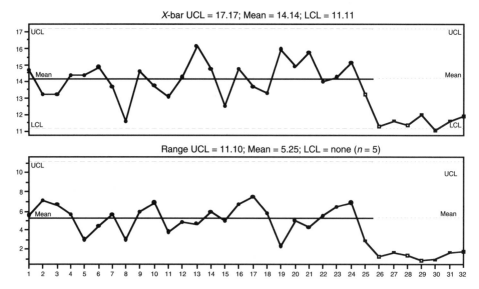

Figure 6.13. Control chart after a change.

Key Points to Remember

H. G. Wells remarked that, one day, statistical thinking will be as necessary for efficient citizenship as the ability to read and write. That "one day" is now.

The basic tools of quality can be used to solve the majority of quality-related problems. They represent an improved method for organizing facts (statistics/numbers) and a better way to determine if change results in improvement.

The Process of Continuous Improvement and Learning

Doing or saying the same thing over and over again and expecting a different result indicates optimism, fear, lack of knowledge, and/or insanity.

Author

Process and Paradigm

The continuous improvement paradigm implies that a problem is never solved because variation is never eliminated. In other words, a problem represents an unacceptable degree of variation, and a solved problem represents an acceptable degree of variation.

The plan-do-study-act (PDSA) cycle represents the continuous improvement process. It is a common sense method that people unconsciously use to resolve any type of problem. The PDSA cycle can be linked to the traditional problem-solving approach:

PDSA	Traditional Problem Solving
Plan	1. Identify the problem (actual situation)
	2. Identify the causes (reasons or excuses)
	3. Develop alternatives/solutions (desired conditions)
Do	4. Implement the best alternative/solution
Study	5. Compare actual results with the desired conditions identified in Step 3
Act	6. Repeat the cycle until you get what you want

The traditional problem-solving process can be further broken down into four phases: problem recognition, decision making, problem resolution, and follow-through. These phases are flowcharted in Figure 7.1.

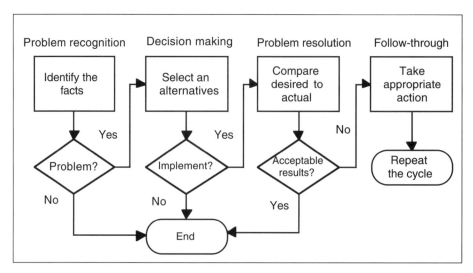

Figure 7.1.   Phases in the traditional problem solving process.

In any type of problem-solving or decision-making process, choices are mandatory and problems are optional. Here is how it works: In the problem-recognition phase, you choose if the facts represent a problem. If you think there is a problem, you proceed to the decision-making phase. At this point, you choose which alternative you think will improve the situation and then decide whether or not to implement it. If you decide to implement the selected alternative, you proceed to the problem-resolution phase. At this time, you take action and determine if the results from the change are acceptable. Finally, in the follow-through phase, you take appropriate action until you get what you want.

The transition from traditional problem solving to continuous process improvement requires an awareness that problems represent outcomes from either a stable or unstable process, causes of problems are due to variation that is either common (usual) or special (unusual), and optimal approaches require the development of a common or shared vision based on the ideal.

The merging of the problem-solving approach and continuous process improvement paradigm results in a refined continuous improvement and learning process. While this process is "not new," it now incorporates new ways of thinking. Table 7.1

TABLE 7.1.	**A Refined Continuous Improvement and Learning Process.**
Plan	Problem recognition **1.** Identify the facts **2.** *Identify and define the process—this includes identifying the requirements and desired/ideal outcomes* **3.** *Plot points to determine if the variation in the process can be predicted* Decision making **1.** Identify causes and/or develop alternatives **2.** Select the best (optimum) alternative **3.** Develop an action plan to implement the selected alternative(s)
Do	Problem resolution **1.** Take action to implement the selected alternative(s).
Study	**2.** Compare actual results with expected outcomes—*share lessons learned*
Act	*Follow-through*—take appropriate action based on the results of the initiative

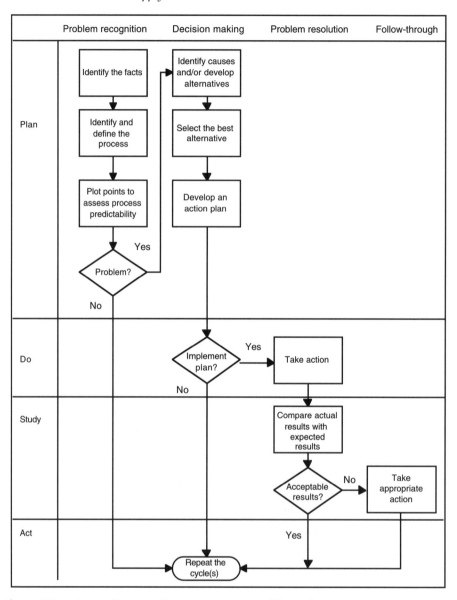

Figure 7.2. A continuous improvement and learning process.

highlights the subtle changes between the old and the new continuous improvement and learning processes (additions are in italics).

Figure 7.2 provides a flowchart of the process, which begins with the selection of an issue and never ends because variation is never eliminated. The application guidelines provide additional details for each step in the process.

TABLE 7.2.	Getting Started with Tools.			
Basic Tools	**Problem Recognition**	**Decision Making**	**Problem Resolution**	**Follow through**
Working with Ideas				
Brainstorming	x	x	x	x
Cause-and-effect diagrams		x		
Flowcharts	x			
Action plan		x		x
Working with Facts				
Run charts	x		x	
Control charts	x		x	
Scatter diagrams			x	
Histograms	x		x	
Pareto charts		x		

How the Basic Tools of Quality Fit In

Although each of the basic tools of quality can be used in any phase of the process, the chart in Table 7.2 provides an introductory guide to the tools commonly used in each phase of the process. When working with groups/teams, additional tools will include group dynamics, facilitation, and meeting management.

Guidelines for Applying the Continuous Improvement and Learning Process

The following guidelines provide specific details for each step in the continuous improvement process, as reflected in Table 7.1.

Problem Recognition

Comparing the desired outcome to the actual outcome can be accomplished by following these steps:

1. *Identify the facts.* Describe the current situation. What is currently happening? What information is currently being used to provide feedback relevant to the issue?

2. *Identify and define the process.* A *flowchart* is a good tool to use to document and communicate actions that are taken or could be taken to achieve intended outcomes. Prior to developing a flowchart, you should:

a. Identify basic needs. What requirements should the process meet?

b. Identify the people who are directly or indirectly affected by the process and identify their respective needs. What products and services are currently being provided to meet these needs? In an organization, for example, direct customers include people who buy the product or service; internal customers are employees; and indirect customers include other stakeholders such as suppliers, families; and community. In Chapter 5, Table 5.1 provides an example of a matrix that can be used to organize this information.

c. Identify desired outcomes. Desired outcomes include what people on all sides of an issue say they want or expect from the process.

d. Identify ideal outcomes (if different from desired). What would people on all sides of the issue agree on as the ideal? Challenge existing mind-sets: What seems impossible today but, if it could be done, would fundamentally improve quality? In other words, what seems impossible but yet is practical? Summarize the ideal outcomes in a vision statement that people working in the process believe is inspiring and achievable. This statement should be brief and should accurately describe what the situation will be like once the vision is achieved. In addition to vision, other common terms used to provide focus for action are *end-state* and *intent.*

e. Ascertain commitment. To help develop commitment to a common or shared vision, record the answers to the following questions: How will you feel or what will the situation be like if the ideal/desired outcome is achieved? What will it be like if the ideal is never achieved? Answers to these questions need to be specific, descriptive, written in the present tense, and frequently reviewed.

3. *Plot points.* What feedback/outcome measures (facts, data, evidence, observations, opinions, benchmarks, etc.) will indicate progress toward the ideal? Develop a *behavior-over-time* (run or control) chart to determine if the process is stable or unstable and to measure progress toward the ideal. Run or control charts are like road signs—they help indicate how many miles you have gone and still need to go.

Decision Making

Developing and selecting an alternative(s) can be accomplished by following these steps:[1]

1. *Identify causes and/or develop alternatives.* In the decision-making cycle, you can either identify causes of the existing problem and then select alternatives, or you can skip identifying causes and go right to developing alternatives. This situation represents different sides of the same coin. For example, if you wanted to work on an issue, such as increasing voter turnout, you could either identify the causes as to why people don't vote, which would help you to identify alternatives, or you could just develop alternatives, like volunteering to register more voters.

A *cause-and-effect diagram* is a useful tool to record causes. Using such a tool, you should:

   a. Identify the causes. What are the possible causes of the problem? Classify these causes according to the amount of control the individual or group has over them. The degree of control can be broken down into:

     • Direct control

     • Some control

     • Little control

   The risks of making changes that will result in improvement are directly proportional to the category of control or power the individual or group has over the respective cause. Generally, the more people involved in resolving the issue who have direct control over one or more of the causes, the higher the odds of success.

---

[1]Adapted from the U. S. Army's tactical decision-making process.

b. Develop alternative solutions for achieving the outcome. Alternatives represent improvement theories (that is, *"If* I do this, *then* this will happen"). Typically, there are two courses of action:

- *Standardize (stabilize/maintain) the process.* This is achieved by developing procedures (rules, laws, or regulations) and then monitoring the process to eliminate special causes when they occur. The improvement cycle for this alternative is referred to as the standardize-do-study-act (SDSA) cycle. The goal in process standardization is to look for ways of minimizing the resources needed to maintain the process. In other words, don't do or say anything that does not add value to the process. This could be as simple as accepting the situation and putting resources on higher priority projects.

- *Improve the process.* The scope of improvement can be either evolutionary or revolutionary. Evolutionary improvement involves incremental changes over time. Revolutionary improvement involves drastic changes that are implemented all at once. Revolutionary improvement is commonly referred to as *starting over from scratch, reinventing, reengineering,* or *redesigning.*

The example of personal body weight illustrates the concepts of standardization and improvement. If you developed a routine for maintaining your existing weight, this would represent *standardization.* If you successfully dropped 10 pounds and kept the weight off, this would represent an *evolutionary* improvement. If you drastically changed your lifestyle, such as adopting a vegetarian diet and exercising every day, this might represent a *revolutionary* improvement.

2. *Select the best alternative.* An optimum solution is one that has a positive impact on everyone affected by the solution both in the short and long term. This is referred to as a *win/win situation.* A *win/lose* or *lose/lose* situation is one in which people affected by the solution believe that it benefits someone else at their expense. For example, consider the American Revolution. At the time, it was an alternative that was perceived as a win for some of the colonists and a loss for those wanting to maintain the status quo. In the long term, the American Revolution is

TABLE 7.3.	Three Alternatives.

Possible Impacts: Win (+); Lose (–)

Solutions	A	B	C	D	Net effect
Alternative 1	+	+	+	+	Win/Win
Alternative 2	+	–	+	+	Win/Lose
Alternative 3	–	–	–	–	Lose/Lose

TABLE 7.4.	Comparing Alternatives.

Comparison Criteria

Ranking: 1 = low; 5 = high	Alternative 1	Alternative 2	Alternative 3
1. Cost	1	3	5
2. Benefits	5	3	1
3. Desire and commitment to change	5	2	4
Total	11	8	10

generally perceived as a win/win situation. Nuclear war is an example of an alternative that most people would agree is a lose/lose situation.

The matrix in Table 7.3 identifies three alternatives that have either a positive or negative impact on other areas (*A* through *D*). An area could represent an individual, group, nation, and so forth.

When selecting the best alternative, you should:

a. Analyze each alternative. What are the advantages (benefits)? What are the disadvantages (concerns)? How will the people who are affected by the change feel about it? What are some of the possible unintended outcomes? Will it unite or divide people? Answers to these questions identify criteria that can be used for comparing alternatives.

b. Compare alternatives. Develop criteria and rank the alternatives. For example, suppose you identified three alternatives and ranked them using the criteria shown in Table 7.4. Based on the ranking, Alternative 1 is the best choice.

3. *Develop an action plan to implement the selected alternative.* An action plan identifies tasks, time lines, resources, and responsibilities.

Problem Resolution

Problems can be resolved by taking the following steps:

1. *Take action to implement the selected alternative(s).*

2. *Compare actual results with expected outcomes.* What was supposed to happen? What actually happened? What went right? What went wrong? What will you do differently next time? If you are monitoring progress with trend or control charts, you need at least seven points either upward or downward, or seven points either above or below the average, to have a statistically significant trend.

Document your success stories, alias "lessons learned," so that they can be used as a future reference and/or to help educate others.

Follow-through

Continuous improvement can be achieved by taking the appropriate action based on the results of the initiative. There must be a balance of standardization and continuous improvement (incremental or radical) for significant and lasting progress. Improvement, like quality, is uniquely defined in each situation, but it usually involves meeting one of the following challenges:[2]

1. *Doing more with less*—Having to meet a higher standard with fewer resources

2. *Doing the same with less*—Having to meet the existing standard with fewer resources

3. *Doing more with the same*—Having to meet a higher standard with the same resources

---

[2]Continuous improvement can also include doing more with more and doing less with less. A company that is increasing its products and services, hiring more employees, or opening more locations to deal with increasing customer demand is an example of doing more with more. An organization that is selling off parts of its business so that it can specialize in a few key areas is an example of doing less with less. Trend and/or control charts of critical performance measures can help validate the category of continuous improvement.

The Continuous Improvement Process at Work

The following examples provide summaries of how the continuous improvement and learning process was applied to improve basketball free throw shooting, to implement a more effective savings and investment process, and to develop this book.

Basketball Free Throw Shooting[3]

1. *Problem recognition.* In a basketball game, when you are in the act of shooting and another player makes physical contact with you, you are given a free shot referred to as a *free throw.* I noticed that my younger son had a stable process for hitting, on average, four out of 10 (40 percent) free throws. He agreed to test a new process to see if his average could be improved. The desired outcome was a higher free throw shooting percentage. I defined an ideal free throw as one that goes in through the middle of the rim, lands on the same spot on the floor every time, and rolls straight back in the shooter's direction after landing.

2. *Decision making.* I believed that a few adjustments (evolutionary improvements) in my son's process would increase his accuracy. The first adjustment was for him to place his right foot at the middle of the foul line (he is a right-handed shooter). Other adjustments required him to visualize the ball going in before he shot and to focus on the front middle of the rim as he shot.

3. *Problem resolution.* These changes to his process resulted in an improvement in practice of an average of 36 percent. During the season, he hit 37 of 52 free throws for an average of 71 percent. While my son's average is nowhere near the world record for consecutive free throws, he was quite happy with his improvement. (Tom Amberry, who was 72 at the time, set the world record by making 2750 free throws over a 12-hour period on November 15, 1993. For practice, he shot 500 free throws a day.)

---

[3]Timothy Clark and Andrew Clark, "Continuous Improvement on the Free-Throw Line." *Quality Progress,* October 1997, pp. 78–80.

4. *Follow-through.* Between seasons, my son went to a basketball camp where one of the instructors advised him to change his process, which he did. During the next season, his free throw shooting average, as well as his other shots, dropped by 20 percent. We then went back to his old process, and his shooting returned to normal.

A Family Investment Strategy

1. *Problem recognition.* When he was old enough, my older son wanted to earn some spending money, so he started his own business of mowing grass, raking leaves, shoveling snow, and babysitting. My son's process for managing money was simple and predictable (that is, stable): Make money; spend money; repeat the cycle. To my son, the fact that he wasn't saving any money was a fact but not a problem; in other words, the process was good enough. As a parent and process owner,[4] however, I felt that the process presented a problem; in other words, the process wasn't good enough. I envisioned what might happen once he was old enough to get his own credit cards. Customers have latent needs, and in this case, my son's latent need was for me and his mom to develop his understanding of the importance of managing money and investing in the future.

2. *Decision making.* Our first attempt to reduce variation was to use all of the standard parent lectures, hoping that these discussions would inspire him to improve his process.

3. *Problem resolution.* After a few months, my wife and I realized that the only time he was saving anything was when we remembered to tell him to make a deposit. We then required him to save 50 percent of everything he earned. We also required him to plot points. When he started keeping records of his earnings and deposits, he began to enjoy seeing the balance in his savings account increase. Money should be enjoyed, but it should also be invested and put to work.

4. *Follow-through.* After a couple of years, the mandatory 50 percent deposit was replaced with a voluntary rate of 10 percent.

---

[4]Technically, parents are the process owners for children who are under the age of 18.

Despite the fact that we changed the standard, he continues to save and invest a minimum of 10 percent and sometimes as much as 100 percent of what he earns.

Motivated by my son's example, my wife and I started plotting points on our own savings history. In his book *The Richest Man in Babylon,* George S. Clason suggests that you save and invest 10 percent of what you earn. In other words, you "pay yourself first" and put your money to work for you.[5] Because of my son's example, our family has been introduced to a whole new paradigm. We are now plotting points on the amount of money our savings are earning.

Writing This Book

1. *Problem recognition.* I put off writing this book for several years for two "good" reasons: I don't like to write, and the only time I have to write is in the evenings and on weekends. I associated massive pain with replacing my free time with something that I did not like doing. To help develop my desire and commitment, I started imagining (visualizing) and writing down all the good things that could happen once the book was completed. This turned out to be an extensive list that I reviewed and updated regularly. The more I reviewed and refined this list, the more committed I became to writing the book.

2. *Decision making.* Two of the biggest barriers that I had were time and a dislike for writing. The alternatives that I selected were to review and refine my list of ideal outcomes and to spend just 2 hours a week on writing.

3. *Problem resolution.* The more I wrote and rewrote, the easier it became. This motivated me to increase the amount of time I spent writing. Also, the more I reviewed my list of ideal outcomes, the more I began to associate pleasure with working on the book, which helped overcome my procrastination. One of my biggest breakthroughs was accepting the fact that the book will never be perfect.

---

[5]George S. Clason, *The Richest Man in Babylon.* New York: Penguin Group, Penguin Books USA Inc., 1955.

4. *Follow-through.* Once a preliminary draft of the book was developed, I gave copies to friends and customers who were interested in helping me improve it. The reader survey questionnaire in Appendix C was also added to solicit feedback and recommendations for future improvements.

Key Points to Remember

Key differences between the old and new problem-solving processes are being aware that problems represent unacceptable degrees of variation and are a result of a process. Processes are either stable or unstable, and reducing process variation requires optimal approaches. Optimization is achieved when quality is improved in one area without making it worse in another. People affected by the process determine if the situation got better or worse.

One of the significant advantage gained by applying the quality methods and tools is that they provide a common language for determining when change results in improvement. Documenting lessons learned and communicating success stories is a great way of helping others who may be working on resolving similar issues. Perhaps the most significant benefit of this technology is that it results in a 100 percent success rate because you always learn something new.

Application of the continuous improvement and learning process creates a chain reaction. Improvement requires change, and change requires action. Action leads to experience, and experience can lead to knowledge. Knowledge of the impacts of the change, to include intended and unintended results, leads to wisdom. Wisdom is increased by taking more action.

Section

3

Why Should I Apply What I Learn?

The Leadership Challenge

Management is doing things right, leadership is doing the right things.

Warren Bennis and Peter Drucker

Given the choice between chaos and order, people generally choose order. Given this desire for order or stability, there are usually more people who accept the status quo (as evidenced by results and not words) than those who want to take action to change it. It is this condition that creates a need for leaders. Change can be managed, but change that results in improvement must be led.

The leadership function requires presentation of an alternative future or end state that inspires the leaders and their followers to take action to achieve it. The end state could be a safer community where doors can be left unlocked at night, or something more common such as a family vacation in which each family member has the chance to choose a day's activity that presents the opportunity for each individual to be a leader and a follower.

As was mentioned at the beginning of this book, change requires the answers to three basic questions:

1. What do I need to know (logical)?

2. How do I apply what I learn (physical)?

3. Why should I apply what I learn (emotional)?

The answers to these questions lie in three critical factors that need to be present in a continuous improvement initiative:

1. What? Develop a conscious awareness and understanding of variation
2. How? Adopt a lead-by-example approach
3. Why? Develop your desire and commitment

It is hoped that this book has given you inspiration, helped you develop a conscious awareness and understanding of variation, and shown you how to apply what you have learned so that you can lead others down the path to continuous improvement. Leading others down the path, however, can be challenging. It requires not only management capabilities, but also leadership abilities.

Differences between Management and Leadership

Management represents the efficiency or science side of quality, deals with the present, and is where we spend most of our time.

TABLE 8.1.	Differences between Management and Leadership.

Quality: Doing the Right Things Right

Management	*Paradigm Shift*	Leadership
If you always do what you always did, you will usually get what you always got.	+	What seems impossible today but, if it could be done, would fundamentally improve quality?
Efficiency	+	Effectiveness
How	+	What and why
Action	+	Vision
Short term	+	Long term
Order	+	Chaos
Science	+	Art
	Continuous improvement	

Routines, habits, and stable processes (commonly referred to as *comfort zones*) are developed to help us improve or maintain efficiencies. This condition is symbolized in the statement: *If you always do what you always did, you will usually get what you always got.* If you don't like what you're getting, then you must make a fundamental change, and this requires leadership. Leadership represents the effectiveness or the art side of quality and focuses on the future. It is symbolized by questions such as: What can be done to improve the situation? or What today seems impossible, but, if it could be done, would fundamentally improve quality? Dr. Robert Shuller suggests asking yourself: What great thing would you attempt if you knew you could not fail?

Table 8.1 contrasts the differences between management and leadership. It's important to note that leadership qualities are additive to management qualities; both are required for continuous improvement.

The challenge of leading others to learn and apply the principles of continuous improvement should not be underestimated. To many people, most of the principles appear to be common sense, nothing new, or just another management fad. In addition, it is relatively easy to develop an academic understanding and knowledge of the quality rhetoric, but true understanding only comes by applying this knowledge. It is similar to the distinction in sports between fans and players. A fan, without ever playing, can be an expert on a particular sport and can even write books about it. But a player, through years of practice and experience, has a level of knowledge and understanding that a fan will never have. Continuous improvement is not a spectator sport. To learn, people have to get in the game.

The following chart, developed by Joiner Associates, Inc., illustrates that on any given issue, the dynamics of change is an unstable process. Leaders represent the avid supporters and, like the active resisters to change, are relatively few in number and represent special causes. The majority of people represent common causes and are neutral, undecided, or persuadeable about change.[1]

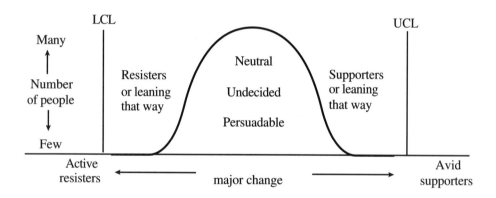

One of the best ways for leaders to get others to support change is to enroll them in a common vision. A *vision* addresses the emotional aspects of change and creates a belief (perception), desire, and an expectation that action will lead to results. The logical aspects of change provide the feedback (facts) that changes are resulting in improvement. Success stories are the fuel that sustains the commitment to the vision.

Enrolling Others in the Vision

Joel Barker, in his video *Discovering The Future: The Power of Vision*, provides the following guidelines for developing a common vision:[2]

1. It must be developed and driven by leaders. Leaders must talk with and listen to their followers, but leaders alone must develop the vision.

2. Leaders must share the vision with their followers, who must agree to support it. Understanding and support equal agreement. This focus improves decision making.

3. The vision must be comprehensive and detailed. It must identify how everyone will contribute and participate.

4. The vision must be positive and inspiring. It must have reach and be worth the effort.

In regard to the role of values (such as truth, honesty, justice, fairness, loyalty, and respect for other people) in a vision, Barker states that values are the way to measure the rightness of the vision's direction. He also emphasizes the importance of combining management (action) and leadership (vision) to achieve individual, organizational, national, and world visions. He summarizes their relationship as follows:[3]

> Action without Vision just passes the time. Vision without Action is just a dream. Action with Vision can change the world.

The Vision Community

In their book *The Leader In You*, Stuart Levine and Michael Crom reinforce the important role that visions have in unleashing the

---

[2]Joel Barker, *Discovering the Future: The Power of Vision*. Burnsville, MN: Charthouse Learning Corp., 1991.

[3]Ibid.

enormous potential all people possess. In the following passage, they share the thoughts of Paul Fireman, chairman of Reebok International, on the importance of building what Joel Barker refers to as the "Vision Community":[4]

> You need to build enrollment. . . . I don't think you can dictate that to people. I don't think you can tell people, "Go. March. Do this." What you need to do is to take the time to enroll people in your thinking, your vision, your dream, your fantasy, whatever it is you're doing. Enroll them. It takes time. It takes effort. It takes continual reinforcement. But you don't dictate. You enroll.
>
> If you enroll one person, then you have a metamorphosis. You change someone, and that person becomes able to enroll ten people. They become able to enroll a hundred people.
>
> . . . It's like the old cowboy movies where the hero was going to make the final battle against the villain and rescue the heroine. As the hero was riding on his white horse, with one other guy next to him, a person joined in from the right. Then ten more on the left. And they keep going until finally, at the end of thirty seconds, there are seven hundred people riding, dust flying, and they're on their way to the final shot.
>
> You can't wait until you call everybody up and say. "Will you join me at River Creek?" You make them want to come along. You ride. You go. And you just suck everybody else with you. The music rises. And you find that when you get there, whether you needed seven hundred or nine hundred, the point is that you're riding. And they want to ride along. You've got to make them want to ride along.

Enrolling people in a common vision can occur not only in the workplace, but also in the communities in which they live.

---

[4]Stuart Levine and Michael Crom, *The Leader In You*. New York: Simon and Schuster, 1993, pp. 46–48.

Community Quality Initiatives

There are many community quality initiatives throughout the United States that are designed to introduce, train, and support people to improve quality. Here are a few of them:

Indianapolis, IN. In Indianapolis, representatives from various quality-related professional associations, local colleges, and the public library are testing a unique prototype that was developed to raise the quality awareness of the general public and to support leaders who want to learn, test, and apply the quality improvement methods and tools. The design of this initiative was inspired by the philosophy of Thomas Jefferson, who believed that if you want an enlightened society, you must have an enlightened citizenry.

Jackson, MI. To support citizens in their community to develop the full potential of the person, family, neighborhood, organization, and institution, the community leaders in Jackson have developed a community transformation initiative that is designed to create competent people through the generation and distribution of wealth, power, beauty, values, and knowledge.[5] They describe these categories as follows:

- *Wealth*—The opportunity for all people to have reasonable resources to meet their own needs and the needs of their families, neighborhoods, organizations, and institutions

- *Power*—The opportunity for all people, families, neighborhoods, organizations, and institutions to share in decisions that affect their well-being

- *Beauty*—The opportunity for all people to find meaning in their lives, to experience belonging in the community, and to enjoy a clean, healthy environment

- *Values*—The opportunity for all people, families, neighborhoods, organizations, and institutions to have the

---

[5]Jackson Comm*U*nity Transformation Project (CTP). For more information, contact the Jackson Community College, 2111 Emmons Rd., Jackson, MI 49201.

means to shape the values and ethics of the community and to have access to resources for resolving conflict

- *Knowledge*—The opportunity for all people, families, neighborhoods, organizations, and institutions to be able to learn and develop their unique talents, skills, and abilities

Oregon. Citizens throughout Oregon are working together to achieve three strategic goals by the year 2010:

- Provide the best educated and prepared workforce

- Maintain the state's natural environment and uncongested way of life

- Maintain a diverse, internationally oriented economy that pays high wages

To accomplish this vision, they have developed performance indicators to measure progress in reaching the three goals. Their work has already led them to win an Innovations in Government award, which is presented by the Ford Foundation and the Kennedy School of Government.[6]

Key Points to Remember

Enrolling others in the vision to continuously improve is not an easy task. It requires not only management capabilities, but also leadership abilities. Perhaps the following quote from Joel Barker provides the best inspiration for quality leaders:

> Action without Vision just passes the time.
> Vision without Action is just a dream.
> Action with Vision can change the world.

---

[6]For more information, contact the Oregon Progress Board, 775 Summer St. NE, Salem, OR 97310, telephone (503) 986-0039, Internet: www.econ.state.or.us/opb/index.htm.

Conclusion

The End . . . and the Beginning?

A jouney of a thousand miles begins with a single step.

Chinese Proverb

Achieving success through quality requires the courage to take action, the knowledge to evaluate the effects of the actions, and a burning desire and commitment to make a *quality* difference.

How do you make a difference? You have already started by reading this book and reviewing the basic principles of quality.

What do you do now? Pick a process that you have the power and responsibility to improve. Your challenge is to reduce variation in one area without making it worse in another. You can start by developing a run or control chart on the outcomes from a personal, family, community, or national process in order to determine if they are predictable and/or to evaluate past or future efforts to improve the situation. This becomes the foundation for your success story and a starting point for supporting others to learn and apply the quality technology.

Why should you do it? You need to ask yourself, "What would my world be like if I helped myself and others to be 'All that I was created to be?'" More importantly, you need to consider what might happen if you don't. Perhaps this unknown philosopher said it best:

> When I was young and free and my imagination had no limits, I dreamed of changing the world. As I grew older and wiser, I discovered the world would not change, so I shortened my sights somewhat and decided to change my country. But it too seemed immovable. As I grew into my twilight years, in one last desperate attempt, I settled for changing my family, those closest to me, but alas, they would have none of it. . . . And now as I lay on my deathbed, I suddenly realize: If only I had changed myself, then by example, I might have changed my family. From their inspiration and encouragement, I would have been able to better my country and who knows—I may have changed the world.
>
> —*From the tomb of a crypt in Westminster Abbey, 1100* A.D.

Appendixes

There will never be a book that is all things to all people, and this one is no exception. Some of the tools discussed, such as histograms and control charts, were presented to offer an introduction to the reader and will require additional study. Appendixes A and B identify books, videos, and other training resources that can help you develop and expand your understanding of quality. Appendix C features a feedback form for you to complete on how well this book has met your expectations.

Selected Bibliography

Books

Barker, Joel Arthur. *Future Edge: Discovering the New Paradigms of Success.* New York: William Morrow and Company, Inc., 1992.

Brassard, Michael. *The Memory Jogger.* Methuen, MA: GOAL/QPC, 1989.

Carr, David K., and Ian D. Littman. *Excellence in Government, Total Quality Management in the 1990s.* Arlington, VA: Cooper and Lybrand, 1990.

Clason, George S. *The Richest Man in Babylon.* New York: Penguin Group, Penguin Books USA Inc., 1955.

Covey, Stephen R. *The 7 Habits of Highly Effective People.* New York: Simon and Schuster, 1989.

Crosby, Phillip B. *Quality Is Free.* New York: McGraw-Hill Book Company, 1979.

Deming, W. Edwards. *The New Economics for Industry, Government, Education.* Cambridge, MA: Massachusetts Institute of Technology, Center for Advanced Engineering Study, 1993.

———. *Out of the Crisis,* 2nd edition. Cambridge, MA: Massachusetts Institute of Technology, Center for Advanced Engineering Study, 1986.

Dobyns, Lloyd, and Clare Crawford-Mason. *Quality or Else: The Revolution in World Business.* New York: Houghton Mifflin Company, 1991.

Frankl, Victor. *Man's Search for Meaning,* 3rd edition. New York: Simon and Schuster, 1984.

Greenleaf, Robert K. *The Servant as Leader.* Indianapolis, IN: Robert K. Greenleaf Center, 1970.

Harrington, H. James. *Poor-Quality Cost.* New York: Marcel Dekker, Inc. and Milwaukee, WI: ASQ Quality Press, 1987.

Herzberg, Frederick, Bernard Mausner, and Barbara B. Snyderman. *The Motivation to Work,* 2nd edition. New York: John Wiley & Sons, 1959.

Hill, Napolean. *Think & Grow Rich.* New York: Random House, Revised edition 1960.

Hounshell, David A. *From the American System to Mass Production, 1800–1932.* Baltimore, MD: Johns Hopkins University Press, 1984.

Ishikawa, Kaoru. *What Is Total Quality Control? The Japanese Way.* Translated by David J. Lu. Englewood Cliffs, NJ: Prentice-Hall, 1985.

Juran, Joseph. M. *Quality Control Handbook,* 4th edition. New York: McGraw-Hill, 1988.

———. *Juran on Leadership for Quality: An Executive Handbook.* New York: The Free Press, 1989.

———. *A History of Managing for Quality. The Evolution, Trends, and Future Directions of Managing for Quality.* Milwaukee, WI: ASQC Quality Press, 1995.

Kuhn, Thomas. *The Structure of Scientific Revolutions,* 2nd edition. Chicago: The University of Chicago Press, 1962.

Mann, Nancy R. *The Keys to Excellence.* Los Angeles: Prestwick Books, 1988.

Maslow, Abraham. *Motivation and Personality,* 3rd edition. New York: Harper and Row, 1987.

McConnell, John. *Analysis and Control of Variation,* 3rd edition. Manly Vale, New South Wales, Australia: Delaware Books, 1987.

———. *Safer Than a Known Way.* Manly Vale, New South Wales, Australia: Delaware Books, 1988.

Osborn, H. F. *Man Rises to Parnussus.* Princeton, NJ: Princeton University Press, 1928.

Peck, M. Scott. *The Road Less Traveled.* New York: Simon and Schuster, 1978.

Robbins, Anthony. *Awaken the Giant Within.* New York: Summit Books, Simon and Schuster, 1991.

Sherkenbach, William W. *The Deming Route to Quality and Productivity: Road Maps and Roadblocks.* Washington, DC: CEEP Press Books, 1988.

Shewhart, Walter A. *Economic Control of Quality of Manufactured Product.* New York: Van Nostrand, 1980.

———. *Statistical Method from the Viewpoint of Quality Control.* New York: Dover Publications, 1986.

Western Electric. *Statistical Quality Control Handbook.* Indianapolis, IN: AT&T, 1985.

Wheeler, Donald J. *Short Run SPC.* Knoxville, TN: SPC Press, 1991.

———. *Understanding Statistical Process Control.* Knoxville, TN: SPC Press, 1992.

Articles, Documentaries, Videos

Barker, Joel A. *Discovering the Future: The Business of Paradigms.* Burnsville, MN: Charthouse Learning Corp., 1990. Video.

———. *Discovering the Future: The Power of Vision.* Burnsville, MN: Charthouse Learning Corp., 1991. Video.

Dobyns, Lloyd. *Volume V: Communication of the New Philosophy,* part of The
  Deming Library. Washington, DC: CC-M Productions, 1987–91.
  Distributed by Films Inc., Chicago, IL.

———. *Volume XIII: America In The Global Market,* part of The Deming Library.
  Washington, DC: CC-M Productions, 1987–91. Distributed by Films Inc.,
  Chicago, IL.

Dobyns, Lloyd, and Frank Reuven. *If Japan Can Why Can't We?* New York:
  NBC News, June 24, 1980.

Provost, Lloyd P., and Clifford L. Norman. "Variation Through the Ages."
  Quality Progress, December 1990, pp. 39–44.

Juran, J. M. Early SQC: "A Historical Supplement." *Quality Progress,*
  September 1997, pp. 73–81.

A Few Sources of Books, Videos, and Training

American Society for Quality (ASQ). Founded in 1946, ASQ is a non-profit educational and scientific society comprised of over 130,000 members with chapters and sections located throughout the world. Its purpose is to create, promote, and stimulate interest in the advancement of quality improvement in industry, education, business, the service sector, and the community. ASQ offers books, training courses, and videos. Its monthly magazine, *Quality Progress,* is an excellent source of information on U. S. and worldwide quality initiatives.

ASQ has developed a program especially for K through 12 schools that is referred to as "Koalaty Kid." This program links ASQ sections and businesses with schools that are interested in applying quality theories, processes, and tools.

ASQ, 611 E. Wisconsin Ave., P.O. Box 3005, Milwaukee, WI 53201, telephone (800) 248-1946 (U.S. and Canada), fax (414) 272-1734, Internet: www.asq.org

GOAL/QPC. GOAL/QPC is a nonprofit organization specializing in research, publishing, and training for quality, productivity, and competitiveness. It offers books, training, and videos. Especially recommended is the *Memory Jogger II—A Pocket Guide of Tools for Continuous Improvement and Effective Planning* and the *Memory Jogger.* There are two versions: one for business and one for education.

GOAL/QPC, 13 Branch St., Methuen, MA 01844, telephone (978) 685-3900, fax (978) 685-6151

Charthouse International Learning Corporation. Charthouse offers two excellent videos by Joel Barker: *Discovering the Future: The Business of Paradigms* and *Discovering the Future: The Power of Vision.*

Charthouse International Learning Corporation, telephone (800) 328-3789, fax (612) 890-0505

The Robert K. Greenleaf Center. The Greenleaf Center's mission is to fundamentally improve the caring and quality of all institutions through a new approach to leadership, structure, and decision making. Servant-Leadership emphasizes increased service to others, a holistic approach to work, promoting a sense of community, and the sharing of power and decision making. The Greenleaf Center offers books, publications, newsletters, videos, and workshops that promote the work of Robert Greenleaf.

The Robert K. Greenleaf Center, 921 E. 86th St., Ste. 200, Indianapolis, IN 46240, telephone (317) 259-1241, fax (317) 259-0560

Simply Better! Simply Better! is a network of employment and training professionals and organizations committed to continuous improvement of their services and outcomes, to customer satisfaction, and to exceptional quality. The Simply Better! network includes private industry councils, private sector service providers, state governments, employment service agencies, and U. S. Department of Labor regional and national offices. The Simply Better! network provides support and materials for organizations interested in meeting the standards of excellence identified by the Malcolm Baldrige National Quality Award criteria.

National office: telephone (202) 219-5585, ext. 222. Internet: http://esc.ttrc.doleta.gov/simplyb/

Customer Feedback

Guidelines. Using a copy of this form, or a blank piece of paper with the questions numbered, please respond to the following questions:

1. Approximately when did you read the book (month and year)? _____

2. Would you recommend this book to someone else?
   Yes _____ No _____

3. Would you buy this book for someone else
   Yes _____ No _____

   Maybe, if _____

	Strongly Disagree			Agree		Strongly Agree
4. This book improved my knowledge and understanding of quality.	0	1	2	**3**	4	5
5. This book provided me with some techniques that I can use to improve the quality in my life.	0	1	2	**3**	4	5

6. What are one or two things you liked most about the book?

7. What are one or two things that could be improved?

8. What are your other comments or recommendations?

9. May I use your name and comments in future promotions of the book?

   No: _____   Yes: _____ If yes, please complete the following:

   Name (please print): _____

   Signature: _____

Please forward to:

Timothy Clark
P.O. Box 19752
Indianapolis, Indiana 46219-9752

Internet: tjclark@asqnet.org

Thank you for taking the time to complete this survey.

Index